A Healing Year

Daily Meditations to Open Your Heart to Forgiveness

Published by One Caring Place
Abbey Press
St. Meinrad, Indiana 47577

Library of Congress Catalog Number
00-103686

ISBN 0-87029-347-8

Printed in the United States of America

A Healing Year

Daily Meditations to Open Your Heart to Forgiveness

By David W. Schell, Ed. D

With contributions by Linus Mundy, and
Denis Robinson, O.S.B.

Abbey Press

To those courageous
individuals who have experienced
the depths of despair,
yet found healing
in forgiveness and a
willingness to show the
rest of us the way.

Introduction

Have you ever said something like the following to yourself or a friend: "As long as I live I'll never forgive so and so....!"? Well, this book presumes we have all known that kind of experience—and that we all know it takes a long, long time to overcome feelings of anger and betrayal. For indeed, very often these feelings are totally justified.

But the truth is, we need to forgive, and we need to seek forgiveness. These are essential in a world where we often do wrong to one another as well as wrong our God who loves us. These are essential in the life of a Christian who has set up the forgiving Christ as the ultimate role-model. And these are essential, if nothing else, in order to know full freedom and peace of heart.

This book is based on the clear premise that forgiveness of others, and forgiveness of self, take *time*. It cannot happen overnight. That's why this book is entitled *A Healing Year to Open Your Heart to Forgiveness.* The title does not imply that all will be forgiven in "just" one year, but that one's heart can begin to be opened up to this noble idea, this lofty—but necessary—goal, over the period of 365 days.

The 365 reflections, essays, and insights in this work come from a rich variety of sources—from the Scriptures, from philosophers, from family and community psychologists, from truck drivers and poets, and truck-driver poets. And they all come from the hearts and souls of individuals who know the imperative of forgiving and being forgiven.

May this book, day by day, open wider the doors and windows of our wounded and wounding hearts…to forgiveness.

Editor's Note: In writing this book, Dr. David Schell has drawn from his experience as a licensed professional counselor. He has also drawn from two of his previous works: *Forgiveness Therapy*, and *Getting Bitter, Getting Better: Choosing Forgiveness for Your Own Good.*

Additionally, portions of this book are adapted from the books, *PrayerStarters on the Way to Forgiveness,* by Denis Robinson, O.S.B., and *PrayerStarters for Dealing With Anger,* by Linus Mundy.

January

"I don't get mad; I get even."

Anger over being victimized can be so deceptive. When we are angry, vengeance is deceptively alluring. Getting even can feel so satisfying. Our emotions dance with glee at the very thought of seeing those who have hurt us suffer in their own agony. After all, those who injure us, either physically or emotionally, should have to pay. Above all else, we speculate, justice must prevail.

Yet, if revenge really worked, if it really cleansed the soul, if it really healed the broken heart, there would be no need for forgiveness. Vengeance neither heals the perpetrator nor the victim; forgiveness has the power to heal both.

2

"To err is human nature; to forgive is human potential."

A woman found in the act of adultery was dragged in shame to where Jesus was teaching. Adding to her humiliation the crowd eagerly anticipated harsh judgment, even hoping for her death. No one voiced the slightest compassion, even though every accuser in the crowd was guilty of the very same offense. No one dared question the conduct of the man discovered with her. Where did he go? Did he also abandon her? Alone, she faced the cruelty of human unforgiveness.

Imagine the liberation the woman must have felt as she was extended forgiveness. Not only was her life spared, her heart was freed to heal. The power of forgiveness overcame human cruelty and restored human dignity.

"When forgiveness seems impossible, start with your big toe."

A woman who has lost two sons to senseless violence understands forgiveness may be a lifelong process. Is it possible to forgive such crimes? If so, how does one begin?

Imagine an angel stirring forgiveness into the warm healing waters of Bethesda. Cautiously test the waters with your big toe. Gradually, submerge your aching heart and hurt feelings. Experience the cleansing strength of forgiveness. To become a forgiving person, start with little offenses. Practice forgiving a rude store clerk. Forgiving an inconsiderate neighbor is a good exercise. Work up to forgiving an insensitive spouse or ungrateful children. Slowly hone your forgiving skills until you are free of bitterness created by major crimes perpetrated against you.

4

"If you think you are going nuts, you might be right."

Anger has a way of causing our emotions to override our better judgment. For instance, no rational person would exhibit fits of rage or scream at defenseless children. In extreme cases, one might even experience or claim temporary insanity.

As an antidote to anger, a forgiving spirit calms the soul. Inner peace tends to displace urges to lash out at others even when they deserve it. Life comes back into balance; sanity is restored.

"If at first you don't succeed, you are no different than anyone else."

A lady worked hard to forgive an abusive husband who left her with small children and no resources. She rebuilt her life a piece at a time. Then, tragically, her estranged husband met an untimely death. Once again she was confronted with the need to forgive. Once again she found serenity. One day while decorating his grave, she found herself enveloped in rage. Discouraged, she felt guilty and unforgiving. Had she been deceiving herself about forgiving this abusive man? No. In the depth of despair, she realized it was time to look beyond herself and forgive him for the misery he had created for their children. Fortunately, she had a lot of practice.

Be patient with yourself. The rewards of forgiveness are worth the effort.

New Directions

An effective technique for helping children learn discipline is called redirection. For instance, two little boys fighting on the playground might be redirected toward helping the teacher build a snowman. Redirection helps children re-channel destructive negative energies into productive positive accomplishments. Soon the two little boys are working together.

Forgiveness, when practiced from the heart, offers a measure of redirection and personal discipline for people of all ages. Energy once consumed in anger may now be re-channeled toward repairing and building relationships. Have you ever wondered why forgiving people have so many friends?

"Don't be penny wise and pound foolish."

Most modern households feel the necessity for budgeting their financial resources. Two-income families have largely replaced the more traditional breadwinner/homemaker roles. Financial problems are a leading cause for divorce. Single parents must be geniuses at budgeting just to survive.

Many of us find we must also budget our emotional resources. Parents and others frequently complain of emotional and physical exhaustion.

Consider forgiveness as an emotional and physical economy measure allowing us to budget these important resources. Forgiving others relieves us of anger and rage which drains us of needed energy. Energy spent in anger is a liability which most of us cannot afford. Loving forgiveness is an asset which pays very attractive dividends.

"Wait 'til your father gets home."

A nearly universal cry among upset mothers who are frustrated with attempts to discipline a recalcitrant child is, "Wait 'til your father gets home!" For many of us, those words created a sense of dread. In vain we hoped our mothers would forget to inform our fathers of our misconduct. Unfortunately, mothers usually have good memory circuits. Paternal discipline was always more certain and occasionally painful.

Children often carry such fears into adult life. For instance, forgiveness may be practiced only as an assurance we ourselves will be forgiven and escape the certain judgment of our Heavenly Father. Perhaps a more mature motive may be forgiving others out of love rather than fear of punishment.

The Load Factor

An airplane pilot must always be aware of the *load factor* or the danger of overloading an airplane. Overloading can be an invitation to disaster. Under some conditions, an overloaded airplane may become airborne. Yet, that same airplane may stall easily in climb or over-stress the wings in a turn.

As we pilot our way through life, we too must be aware of the *load factor* or the danger of overloading our hearts with excess anger. Such overloading is invitation to disaster. Angry people are often able to fly but risk stalling or becoming over-stressed in the climbs and turns of life.

Forgiveness lightens the *load factor* we place on the human heart. Forgiveness renews strength that we might mount up with wings as eagles!

10

"Forgiveness means bending without breaking, being strong enough to withstand the heavy weight of injury, but resilient enough to recover."

—Forgiveness Therapy

Refusing to forgive others who violate us produces a hard heart. Most often, hard hearts are protective. A hard heart may be nothing more than an effort to withstand injustice and unfairness. Unfortunately, hard hearts are rigid and may eventually shatter.

A forgiving heart may also be an aching heart. After all, injury hurts! But a forgiving heart is resilient. One might be terribly injured but not shattered. A resilient heart remains intact and receptive to the healing forces of forgiveness.

"I'm going out and eat worms."

Most of us recall times as children when we felt friendless, unloved, and unwanted. A few of us may recall a line from an old verse, "Nobody likes me, everybody hates me, I'm going out and eat worms." As adults, we experience similar situations and feelings. Sometimes these lonely feelings seem like the only friends we have left.

At such times our natural reaction is to lash out at others. After all, they have been insensitive to our rights and feelings. They have failed to extend to us the understanding we deserve. It is easy to become unforgiving and embittered. Indeed, human beings can be thoughtless, inconsiderate, and even cruel. There are no perfect human beings. Can we afford to drive everyone away?

Be forgiving; it beats eating worms!

12 *"He who steals my purse steals trash."*

—Shakespeare

During a garbage strike in New York, trash and garbage began piling up in the city. One enterprising New Yorker packaged his refuse in gift-wrapped boxes and left the boxes in his unlocked car. Before long, thieves opened the car and stole the boxes.

Under normal circumstances, theft is a hard offense to forgive. Stealing is a desecration of our individual rights, our personal boundaries. We are left feeling violated, powerless and angry.

Forgiveness may help us put such losses into perspective. One indeed may suffer the loss of possessions. In most cases we are helpless to prevent such losses. Yet, forgiveness prevents the theft of our personal dignity, inner peace, and tranquility. When compared to these treasures all else is trash in gift-wrapped boxes.

"Hindsight is always 20/20."

A forty-year-old man lamented, "If only I had known my father was having a heart attack, I would have rushed him to the hospital. He was so afraid of hospitals. I thought I was doing the right thing. I feel so guilty, I should have known!"

Most of us tend to torture ourselves over and over when our good intentions do not turn out well. We castigate ourselves and fail to realize we did the best we knew how to do with the information we had at the time. We may completely overlook the fact our heart was in the right place all along.

In such cases forgiveness is not really necessary. We have done nothing wrong. While we may feel grief, we may also take comfort in knowing we did our best.

14 *"Will the hurting ever go away?"*

Forgiveness may as well be a concept from outer space when one is hurting due to the thoughtless, inconsiderate, or malicious behavior of someone who has left us either emotionally or physically damaged. Under most circumstances, pain inevitably remits to the point one can resume normal living. Yet, in the midst of pain, time seems to stop. We convince ourselves anguish and heart-break will never end. We become especially vulnerable to bitterness and hostility. Some even deplore living.

In the throes of pain, begin preparing your heart to forgive the person who has hurt you. Remind yourself pain is not forever. Forgiveness will hasten your healing. The pain you feel now may be over long before the bitterness you might acquire leaves your soul.

"To thine own self be true"

—Shakespeare

Sensitive people may hurt more, simply because they are more sensitive. They may be hurt more frequently and experience pain more deeply. Sensitive people seldom live in black and white; they live in vivid technicolor!

Unfortunately, some sensitive people become callous and unfeeling in an attempt to protect themselves from emotional wounds. Color fades from their lives. Such people end up being untrue to themselves. But the loss does not stop there. The world needs more sensitive, caring people.

Forgiveness permits sensitive people to continue caring but also allows a measure of protection. Forgiveness does not require one to subject themselves to abuse. Open your heart to forgiveness and to thine own self be true.

16

"When I thought to know this, it was too painful for me."

—The Psalms

Many fail to forgive, claiming they cannot forgive until they understand the motives of the offender. Unfortunately, such understanding may never be accomplished. Understanding the human capacity for malicious behavior may well exceed the limits of human comprehension. For instance, serial killers are universally unable to rationally explain their own compulsions.

Indeed, understanding an offense may elicit compassion and therefore facilitate forgiveness. Yet, some crimes are so painful, understanding remains elusive. Fortunately, one need not have understanding to experience compassion anymore than one needs to understand electrical engineering to turn on a light bulb.

Sometimes understanding is painfully beyond our reach; forgiveness is always at hand.

"I know I've forgiven; so why am I still hurting?"

Simply because healing takes longer than forgiving. Forgiving makes healing possible. By removing contaminants and sterilizing the wound, an injury is allowed to heal without infection.

Forgiveness and healing are not the same. Forgiveness is a prerequisite for healing. Major wounds may take a long time to heal. Deep wounds may even require periodic draining. But healing cannot take place as long as emotional debris remains in the wound and is allowed to fester.

In addition, forgiveness itself may be a painful process. But so is any form of surgery. Tend to your wounds; keep them clean. Healing will come.

18

"Men are wise in proportion not to their experience but to their capacity for experience."

—George Bernard Shaw

Experts tell us children learn most everything they will ever know by age seven. Mark Twain once commented, at age 14, he thought his father was the dumbest creature on earth. At age 21, he was amazed how much his father had learned in seven years.

In reality, children are often more knowledgeable than their parents or even their teachers. Some children have an astounding command of technology. Why then do children need parents and mentors? Simply because they do not have the experience needed to develop wisdom.

Each generation must look to elders who have experienced back-stabbing, yet have found the wisdom of forgiveness. Experience tempered with the wisdom of forgiveness is a worthy heritage.

"When a man's pursuit gradually makes his face shine and grow handsome, be sure it is a worthy one."

—William James

Inwardly, most of us would like to look like movie stars. Young women often starve themselves hoping to look like popular models. Some diet so severely they jeopardize their health. A few die in their vain attempt to be beautiful. Boys often take dangerous drugs hoping to build their bodies into magnificent muscular specimens.

As one approaches middle age we may desperately attempt to fight off aging in hope of maintaining perpetual youth. Plastic surgeon Maxwell Maltz's comments on therapeutic forgiveness may have particular relevance. He wrote, "You'll actually look . . . five or ten years younger in appearance after removing old emotional scars."

Practice forgiveness; it's good for your complexion.

"I dunno."

A seventeen-year-old developed the habit of reacting to problems with a reflexive, "I dunno." His "I dunno" approach to life restricted his ability to think. He remained emotionally stunted, subject to unpredictable episodes of rage. His anger was evident to everyone but himself. He was referred for counseling. The counselor listened patiently as the young man repeatedly echoed, "I dunno." Finally, the counselor responded, "Young man, I believe you. I'm convinced you really don't know what is troubling you. Let me walk with you into your heart until we *know* why you are so angry."

The counselor's advice was a turning point. Once the young man discovered the source of his anger he was able to forgive. "I dunno" suddenly dropped from his vocabulary.

We all want to be liked and need to be loved. Yet, most of us experience times of loneliness. For instance, a lonely teenager complained he was the only student in his class who had not at least experimented with drugs or alcohol. Though tempted, he refused to put his life and future at risk for the sake of social acceptance. This brave young man was not only shunned, he was ridiculed.

Fortunately, this exceptional adolescent found forgiveness opens the door to inner peace and inner peace inspires new perspectives. Suddenly, this forgiving teenager realized he would make a very good friend to anyone who would accept his offer of friendship. Not only did he come to a deeper appreciation of his own standards, he found new friends.

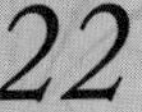

22 *"Praise God, and pass the ammunition!"*

Many of us are reluctant to forgive because we fear forgiveness means forgetting and forgetting would deplete our arsenal. We may reason it is best to keep our powder dry and canon fodder packed tight. We become like powder-kegs ready to explode at the slightest provoking spark.

Of course, the real question is, *Can we forget* even if we choose to do so? Not likely. Important memories seem to be imprinted on permanent neural circuits in the brain. These circuits tend to remain intact unless destroyed by disease, brain injury, or perhaps a lobotomy, none of which are acceptable for voluntarily deleting unwanted memories.

Fortunately, forgiveness does not require forgetting. Forgiveness decontaminates by removing our own anger. The fuse is removed. The powder keg is safe.

"Children start out by loving their parents. Then they like them. Then they judge them. And sometimes they forgive them."

—Oscar Wilde

All parents make mistakes and some of those mistakes may seriously impair our development. Many children never overcome these impediments and grow into dysfunctional adults who repeat the same mistakes with their own children. Yet, other children grow into strong adults who parent their children with love, strength, and direction. Such differences are often observed among adult siblings who have become parents but who were raised in the same home.

Children and adults who choose to forgive their parents are more apt to become better parents themselves. They are courageous people who have grown beyond blaming their parents and have assumed responsibility for their own emotional and spiritual well-being.

Serenity

A friend once jested, "I wish I were an alcoholic so I could pray the Prayer of Serenity." Of course the Prayer of Serenity is a worthy guide for anyone. We all seek inner composure.

Anger is not a pleasant feeling. Indeed, some resort to alcohol hoping to abate intense storms of rage. The more intense the anger the more elusive serenity becomes. Consider that forgiveness allays anger and prepares one's heart to receive the rich bounty of serenity. With that in mind, pray:

God grant me the serenity
To accept the things
I cannot change.
Courage to change
The things I can.
And wisdom
to know the difference.

"For when I am weak, then I am strong."

—St. Paul

There is strength in anger. A lot of it! The more angry we become, the more adrenaline is pumped into our bloodstreams. Enraged people are often capable of phenomenal feats of strength. In fits of rage property may be destroyed; people may be injured or even killed.

Forgiveness means letting go of anger which also means sacrificing the power of adrenaline. The very thought of sacrificing such power may strike fear in our hearts. Without anger we risk feeling empty and feeble.

Yet, forgiveness brings a renewed strength; the quiet strength needed to maintain a balanced life. Is forgiveness a sign of weakness? Perhaps. But consider the words of one of the strongest men in history who discovered when he was weak, he was truly strong.

26

"Hear my voice O God in my complaint."

—Psalm 64:1

There are times when we might be angry with God. This is often the hardest anger to admit. It is not rare to blame God at times for things that happen to us: the loss of a loved one or friend, a failed relationship. From a young age, however, we are instructed that we should not be angry, especially with God. Yet the Psalmist was frequently irate and frustrated with God. He had questions and complaints for God. He did not always understand or appreciate God's ways.

We frequently deny anger and go through life as though everything is fine. Can God understand my anger? Can God understand even when I feel angry with Him? Of course He can. God is compassionate with our anger because He loves us so intensely.

Many of us grew up hearing endless sermons on our need to be forgiven. Some of us became experts at feeling guilty. Therapeutic forgiveness is an interesting subject because the focus is on what others have done to us rather than what we have done to others.

To be sure, we all have needs to be forgiven. But receiving forgiveness may not necessarily prepare us to practice forgiveness. To practice forgiveness we must be willing to rise above the malicious behavior of others. We must learn to forgive even when offenders are not penitent. We must confront our own inner pain. Such struggles do not seem like a lovely idea until we begin feeling renewed strength and healing.

28

"Judge not until you have walked a mile in my moccasins."

Most forgiving people have learned to be patient with those yet struggling in the mire of unforgiveness. Since the journey from agony to forgiveness can be difficult and often fraught with setbacks, walking with forgiving people may offer support and direction.

No crime is so heinous, no victimization so traumatic that someone else has not successfully walked the path you now face. Seek out those who have walked through your valley and experienced triumph on the other side. Do not fear to reach out to them, for someday someone will reach out to you. Share your moccasins for you will have found the way.

"The highest reward for man's toil is not what he gets for it but what he becomes by it."

—John Ruskin

Forgiveness can mean a lot of hard work. Sorting out angry and hurt feelings can leave us exhausted. Indeed we might ask, Why should I forgive? What would I get out of it? Are the rewards worth the effort? These are perfectly legitimate questions.

In material terms, the toil of forgiveness pays nothing. In monetary terms, forgiveness is a waste of time and energy.

The highest reward is not what we get out of forgiveness but what we become by it. Such rewards are attractive when we become better people, when our lives come back into balance, when we sleep better and smile more. Moreover, these rewards are not subject to income tax.

30

"I find the great thing in the world is not so much where we stand as in what direction we are moving."

—Oliver Wendell Holmes

Everyone experiences anger, rage, frustration and hurt. These powerful feelings provide convenient platforms for taking an unforgiving stand. Taking such a stand is counterproductive and lacks direction. Conversely, taking a forgiving stand provides direction through difficult circumstances.

For example, an airplane pilot uses a heading indicator to keep on course. Before taking off, the heading indicator is set to correspond with the magnetic compass. The pilot has taken a stand. Periodically, the heading indicator is corrected while in flight.

Forgiveness is much like a pilot's heading indicator. We take a stand and set the course. We are also responsible for making corrections needed to persist in a positive direction.

"He who cannot forgive breaks the bridge over which he himself must pass."

—George Herbert

People who claim they cannot forgive, usually mean they will not forgive. Forgiveness requires effort; seething in hurt is miserable but not difficult. People, like electricity, tend to short circuit and take the course of least resistance. Shorted electrical circuits cause fires, blown fuses, and loss of power. Short-circuited people may be unforgiving, alone, and ultimately powerless.

Building bridges is more difficult than destroying them. Building requires effort; destruction is not difficult.

Building bridges of forgiveness allows us to cross over the troubled waters of our souls. Forgiveness bridges may span the chasms of broken relationships. Bridges of forgiveness permit us to maintain a lifeline with the divine spark of our humanity.

FEBRUARY

"What if I cry?"

A gracious lady attending a week-long seminar on therapeutic forgiveness came to the instructor during the first break and anxiously said, "I'm afraid I've chosen the wrong seminar. I carry so much anger, I know I will break down and cry."

Encouraged by the instructor, she continued the seminar. Did she cry? Yes, profusely. For several days she cried and spewed out rage over a drunk driver who had killed her son.

Later, she came again to the instructor and said, "I'm so embarrassed. I couldn't keep from crying. It just had to come out." The instructor replied, "Jesus wept." The lady smiled. Light came back into her eyes. Healing had begun.

2 *Our Inner Child*

Psychotherapists sometimes encourage us to become reacquainted with our *inner child.* Our inner child characterizes those memories and feelings we experienced as children but now reside deep inside. Occasionally, our inner child comes out to play. We have fun. Once in a while, our inner child acts like a spoiled brat. No one has fun. By examining our inner child we may gain insights into more effective living. For example, compared to adults, children have more difficulty understanding the need to forgive. But once they understand, forgiveness comes easily. Adults easily understand the need to forgive, but have more trouble putting forgiveness into practice. By becoming acquainted with our own inner child we might learn to exercise adult reasoning but practice child-like forgiveness.

"Time will heal all wounds." Really?

No, time alone will not heal our emotional wounds, but healing indeed takes time. If time healed all wounds, forgiveness would not be necessary. Time is not a healing agent. Healing is contingent on what one does with time. Time offers the opportunity to grasp and express our grievances.

In some cases time can actually make our injuries worse. Time may offer no more than an extended opportunity to simmer in the juices of unresolved wrath.

Forgiveness empowers us to use time wisely. Time allows us the luxury of reevaluating our bitterness, to decompress our emotions, to clear our minds. Time proffers hope. When hurts are forgiven, time facilitates the patience to heal.

Where does anger go?

Emotionally, anger is a form of energy. Physicists tell us energy does not disappear; it only changes form. For instance, energy from the sun may be converted into warming the earth for growing trees. Photosynthesis stores energy from the sun which is converted back into heat when wood is burned as fuel.

Anger is an insidious emotion because the energy of anger may take many forms. The most obvious form of anger is experienced when we lash out at others. However, anger may also be turned inward and feed depression. One expert described depression as frozen rage.

Fortunately, anger may also be forgiven. Forgiveness converts the energy of anger into thawing the heart and quieting the disturbed soul.

"A begging dog is never full."

Internal anger can have an insatiable appetite. In some cases anger can develop such an appetite our emotional and spiritual strength is completely depleted. Unresolved rage is like a black hole in space, ever consuming; never returning.

Feeding a begging dog only reinforces the dog's determination to beg. Likewise, when anger is fed it is reinforced and becomes even more demanding. We run the risk of becoming fixated on revenge and retaliation. In some situations we might find ourselves steeped in self-pity. Such obsessions feed relentlessly on our souls, leaving us empty.

Forgiveness sustains the soul. Our appetite for reprisal is transformed into a passion for spiritual and emotional nourishment. Such nourishment is not exactly cuisine, but tastes a lot better than dog food.

6

"Don't give up. Moses was a basket case, too."

—Sign on a church in Clanton, AL

A young lady found herself engulfed in guilt and deeply depressed. Her mind tormented her day and night, replaying accusations of past mistakes. She longed for the love she thought she shared with a young man who abandoned her leaving her to suffer in shame. She described herself as, "a complete basket case." With guidance, this dauntless young lady refused to give up. Finding new strength, she began assuming responsibility for her own feelings. Assuming such responsibility was difficult but proved to be a foundation for forgiving herself. Slowly, as she expanded her forgiveness to include the young man, her depression lifted.

Moses floated in a basket until he was rescued by a princess. This young lady was rescued by the power of forgiveness and found she was a princess.

"Life is never perfect and often unfair. Forgive life's inevitable failures."

—Forgiveness Therapy

The only real guarantee in life is that there are no guarantees. While most of us believe in fairness and work to practice fairness, unfairness abounds. For instance, natural disasters strike without discernment. No one escapes being treated unfairly at least from time to time. Social unfairness is often directed toward those in poverty who can least afford the cost.

When angered by unfairness, think of people like Helen Keller who possessed a brilliant mind imprisoned in an imperfect body deprived of seeing and hearing. In spite of devastating unfairness, she overcame these obstacles and has inspired the world. In light of her magnificent accomplishments, maybe forgiving life's inevitable failures might not be as difficult as we might think.

8

"Forgive yourself for what you regret doing and for what you wish you had done, for not being fully yourself and for being only yourself."

—Forgiveness Therapy

A desperate teenager wrote, "Why can't I make peace with myself? I express my feelings by hitting something, yelling, crying, or cutting my wrist. Sometimes I scare myself because I don't know what I will do next."

In short, this bewildered teenager has not learned to be human. When human beings do wrong, guilt feelings are normal. For instance, it is perfectly natural to feel guilty for hurting others. Those who do not feel guilt for such behaviors are seriously impaired. Prisons are full of people who feel guilty only when they are caught. A guilty conscience is a signal to change our behavior. But once we have corrected our behavior, guilt has accomplished its purpose. It is time to forgive ourselves, give up the guilt, and go back to being fully ourselves.

"Do not let the sun go down on your anger."

—Ephesians 4:26

There may not be a 24-hour statute of limitations on being angry—some difficult situations take a long time to resolve—but there always comes a time to lay down your anger and carry on with life.

If you have the pervasive feeling of being "stuck" in anger, you probably are. To break the logjam, do the hardest thing: Let it go. Give yourself (and/or another "offender") permission to be human; give God permission to be God. This short prayer may help:

Dear God, please keep me from becoming frozen in the pain, from staying focused on the offender, and victimizing myself over and over. It just lets the original pain repeat itself with the same impact. Help me to start fresh, with you who are Mercy and Forgiveness and Love Itself, there at my side. Amen.

10

"The most consummately beautiful thing in the universe is the rightly fashioned life of a good person."

—George Herbert Palmer

Human beings are given the power to design, to even become architects, of our own lives. Foremost among our designing tools is the capacity to make choices. Yet, this power is a two-edged sword. Choices can be used to fashion or destroy.

The power to make choices also gives us a measure of control. To be sure, we cannot control many of the forces which shape our destiny. For instance, we cannot control other people. We may feel helpless to change adverse circumstances. Yet, we may indeed assume control over the quality of person we choose to become.

Martin Luther King, Jr., once remarked, "It is always the right time to do the right thing." If not always the easy choice, forgiveness is always the right choice. To choose less is to mar the beauty of our destiny.

"Success is to be measured not so much by the position one has reached in life as by the obstacles which he has overcome while trying to succeed."

—Booker T. Washington

A 22-year-old mother of three grew up in a severely cruel home where she was unspeakably abused. Her misfortune compounded as she was moved from one abusive environment to another.

As an adult, she worked hard to forgive her parents along with a host of others who had heartlessly exploited her. She found forgiving those who had turned a deaf ear to her cries for help expressly laborious. One day she wrote in her journal, "I just hope I'll be able to be close to my children when they grow up. I will be there for them when and where they need me. I love my father, my kids, my husband, and my God, always."

This quiet, forgiving young mother will not likely achieve fame or wide recognition. Contemplate her accomplishments. Is she a successful person?

12

"The measure of success is not whether you have a tough problem to deal with, but whether it's the same problem you had last year."

—John Foster Dulles

All of us have times when we become angry, hurt, and perhaps debilitated. Frequently, these experiences are caused by the malicious, thoughtless, or careless actions of others. Most of us know by experience what it means to be emotionally knocked flat on our backs.

When flat on our backs, resolving anger can seem futile. This is fertile soil for depression and lethargy. Furthermore, problem-solving skills tend to atrophy unless practiced. A year later we might still be out of commission.

Fortunately, when we are flat on our backs, if we will open our eyes, we will find ourselves looking up. By opening our hearts, forgiveness empowers us to dispel anger, look around, set new goals, get up, and begin rebuilding.

"Conviction is worthless unless it is converted into conduct."

—Thomas Carlyle

To espouse forgiveness does not make us a forgiving person. To be sure, actions speak louder than words. What we think is relatively innocuous. What we believe is the fuel which drives our behavior.

Nonetheless, to talk about forgiveness is at least a start. Talking about forgiveness is an indication one knows the right thing to do. But talking about forgiveness is no assurance we will actually put it into practice. Talk is cheap; forgiveness has value beyond measure.

Forgiveness must first be an acceptable idea in our thinking. As an acceptable idea, it must become a conviction incorporated into our beliefs. Finally, as a cherished conviction, forgiveness must be translated into our actions.

14 *"God has put something noble and good into every heart which His hand has created."*

—Mark Twain

No doubt, the capacity to forgive is a noble and good quality instilled into every human heart. Not only has God given us the capacity to forgive, He has given us His own forgiveness. Love and forgiveness are lessons God has chosen to teach us by example.

The ability to forgive is often confused with a willingness to forgive. Refusing to forgive others is a violation of our own integrity.

Though often eclipsed by feelings fluctuating from irksome irritation to rampaging rage, the ability to forgive remains in the human heart. Even when deeply buried, the capacity to forgive is our assurance of a Higher Power and a reminder of His forgiveness. For when all else fails, we may turn to our Creator who will reconnect us to that which is noble and good in our own hearts.

"Man is born broken. He lives by mending. The grace of God is glue!"

—Eugene O'Neill

People are in fact broken and that, no doubt, is tragic. Yet, refusing to mend ourselves is even more tragic.

To be sure, the capacity to forgive is a glue given to each of us. We restore meaning to our lives by mending ourselves back together. Forgiveness is also a glue which mends broken hearts and broken relationships.

Sometimes we are broken into very small pieces. But each piece is precious, a part of ourselves and worthy of repair.

When forgiveness seems a formidable task, remember as human beings we are not replaceable. Our only choices are to repair or remain broken. Repairing may be tedious but we will never run out of glue.

16

"I am an old man and have known a great many troubles, but most of them have never happened."

—Mark Twain

Age tends to change our perspectives on life. Some people become embittered; others mellow. The practice of forgiveness can make a substantial difference. Violations which seemed so traumatic become distant memories lost in the mist of passing time. Some trials even become humorous.

Begin practicing forgiveness early in life. Young adults who practice forgiveness grow into forgiving senior citizens.

Aging is an inevitable process. No one welcomes the aches, pains, and limitations brought on by aging. Great care should be taken to avoid bringing unforgiven conflict into our golden years. Learning early to forgive ourselves and others will assure our golden years are at least gold plated.

"What we have accepted into our hearts and made a permanent part of ourselves is given back in times of trial."

—Fulton J. Sheen

Everyone has occasion to forgive others, not once but many times throughout life. Unfortunately, we may find ourselves ill-prepared when forgiveness is needed most. The spirit of forgiveness can and should be made a part of ourselves. The art of forgiveness ought to be cultivated and practiced until it becomes automatic. Incorporating forgiveness into our hearts is to make it a permanent part of our lifestyle. Forgiveness is not something we do one time; it becomes a reflexive response. Routine forgiveness of everyday offenses is simply practice which prepares us for major hurts. By opening our hearts to forgiveness, we prepare for times of trial which might otherwise crush us. The power of forgiveness in the human heart determines whether we live as victims or victors.

18 *"What life means to us is determined not so much by what life brings to us as by the attitude we bring to life; not so much by what happens to us as to our reaction to what happens."*

—Lewis L. Dunnington

Perhaps no attitude shapes life as much as an attitude of love. A major component of love is the ability to extend and practice forgiveness. The ability to forgive when we have been violated is a reflection of love for ourselves, for others, and our Creator.

Life is not always fair. People are not always fair. We cannot live our lives based on the assumption we will be treated fairly. Fairness is a beautiful concept but often set on a very unstable foundation. Loving and forgiving people are sometimes horribly mistreated or confronted with overwhelming life circumstances. Profound love endures all things because forgiveness is an essential component of love.

"Nothing happens to anybody which he is not fitted by nature to bear."

—Marcus Aurelius

The scope of forgiveness is only limited by the boundaries we ourselves set. Murder, rape, and severe child abuse are often considered beyond the scope of forgiveness. Yet, some people are able to forgive these outrageous atrocities. Why? They seem to expand the boundaries of forgiveness as far as necessary to regain their hold on life.

Forgiveness should never be confused with efforts to justify such crimes or to allow ourselves or anyone else to be subjected to victimization. Nor does forgiveness imply perpetrators should escape the consequences of their inhumanity.

Deep in the human heart is the ability to forgive. That ability is limited only by boundaries we have set for ourselves. Fortunately, we have also been fitted by nature with the ability to expand those boundaries.

20 *"Don't just stand there; do something."*

A young chaplain in training was assigned duties on the wards of a state mental hospital. Eager to serve but uncertain what to do, the young chaplain sought advice from his wise and experienced professor.

The wise professor thought for a moment and then replied, "Get a shovel and dig." Then the professor went on to explain, "The needs are so great it makes little difference where you dig. Whatever you do for these people will be more than they have now."

The professor's advice calls to mind the Great Teacher who was described as one who went about doing good. There is no elaboration on what He did, only the fact he did good.

A forgiving spirit helps equip us to do good things. To practice, teach and model forgiveness is a worthy shovel. Don't just stand there; do something.

"I'll think on that tomorrow."

—Scarlet O'Hara, in Gone with the Wind

Coping with anger and hurt is not usually easy. Most of us would prefer to ignore these feelings and hope they will somehow vanish. Indeed, they often seem to disappear. But do our negative feelings really disappear, or do they simply get lost in the labyrinth of other unresolved feelings and become unrecognizable? Professional therapists call this mechanism "suppression." Most of us think of it as "stuffing" our feelings deep inside.

Whether suppressing or stuffing our feelings, this Scarlet O'Hara approach to coping seldom works over an extended period of time. Of course, suppression may be a lot easier than forgiving. That is why stuffing is so appealing.

Remember it is always better to forgive today than to wait and think on it tomorrow.

22

"My hatred will change or punish the offender, and the greater my hatred the more the offender will suffer."

Recovering alcoholics have a familiar saying, "It's the stinkin' thinkin' that causes the drinkin'." Indeed, this is true. Stinkin' thinkin' causes a lot more than drinking. It causes stinkin' living as well.

Stinkin' thinkin' is not only malodorous, it is illogical. Rational thought teaches us the measure of our hatred or pain may have no direct bearing on the offender. We might hope they would feel guilty and stop hurting us or at least apologize. But there is no assurance they will feel anything at all. In some cases, the offender may be gleeful at the thought of our pain. After all, perpetrators are notorious for their own brand of stinkin' thinkin'.

Forgiveness corrects our thinking and heals our feelings. We are not responsible for changing or punishing those who hurt us. Somehow, forgiving people seem to smell better.

"Sorting our emotional garbage is wearisome; hauling it away is exhausting."

In tears a young woman cried, "What will I do? I keep thinking about how much he hurt me. I don't seem to be able to get over it!"

Many of us delay our healing by holding onto our garbage. We may trash self-defeating patterns of behavior or destructive relationships only to find ourselves chasing down the street after the garbage truck to retrieve the trash we discarded.

Forgiveness allows us to forgive ourselves and let go of the debris of shattered relationships, betrayal, victimization, and outrage. Sorting out such residue may not be easy. Anger, hate, and hostility are powerful forces. Living without these feelings may seem to threaten our very identity. But then who wants to be known for chasing the trash truck down the street?

24 *Justice only rights wrongs. Forgiveness heals. Forgiveness transcends justice.*

Justice is a necessary and wonderful concept. But for many, it is only a concept. A seasoned child therapist once remarked, "Over the course of my career I have often seen eight-year-olds who have suffered more injustice than most octogenarians have experienced in a lifetime."

Many of these children will never know a balance of justice. Some will be scared for the rest of their lives. A few will grow up and perpetrate injustice on others.

Forgiveness, too, is a necessary and wonderful concept. For many, forgiveness also remains only a concept. While justice is often out of our control, forgiveness always remains a viable choice.

Victims certainly have a right to bitterness, but victims also have a right to forgive.

The rights of victims are frequently overshadowed. A common complaint lodged against the criminal justice system is that the rights of criminals often seem to supersede the rights of those who suffer as victims of their crimes. For example, violent criminals may be back out on the streets before their victims are discharged from the hospital.

In an effort to focus on victim's rights, emphasis is sometimes placed on the helplessness and unfairness experienced by victims. To be sure, victims have a right to these feelings—even the right to harbor bitterness.

Forgiveness goes beyond victimization. Victims also have the right to forgive. Victimization elicits pity; forgiveness empowers us to rebuild. Be sure to exercise your full rights.

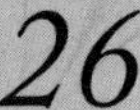

Blame is not therapeutic. If it were, there would be no need for forgiveness.

Blaming others for our emotional conflicts, hurts, and angers is a normal attempt to make ourselves feel better. At least, blaming allows us to experience the false comfort of self-pity. Seldom considered is the fact blaming others places control of our feelings in the hands of those who have mistreated us.

While clarifying our need to forgive is important, blaming is nonproductive and often counterproductive. Steeping ourselves in blame only serves to reinforce and strengthen our negative emotions. Self-pity is not sustaining.

To cease blaming is to assume responsibility for our own feelings. This is an important maneuver toward implementing forgiveness. Blaming and forgiving cannot coexist in our hearts. Blaming is a halting attempt to feel better; forgiveness gets the job done.

Out of sight, out of mind.

Very small children believe if an object or person is out of sight, that object or person does not exist. That is why they enjoy playing peek-a-boo. People seem to appear and disappear just by opening or closing their eyes. As children get older they learn that objects and people continue to exist even when they are out of sight.

Some adults continue playing peek-a-boo with deep emotional wounds. Forgiveness is never accomplished as their wounds remain hidden.

Of course, closing our eyes does not really make our pain go away. Eventually we must learn to open our eyes. Out of sight does not mean out of heart. But by opening our hearts to forgiveness, we may also open our eyes to our wounds and find new inspiration for spiritual and emotional development.

28 *Our hearts go wherever we go.*

In the United States approximately one out five families move every year. New homes, new schools, new churches, new communities, and new friends may signify new hope and new beginnings.

Unfortunately, these new beginnings are often tarnished or lost among the stresses, pains, and problems we failed to leave behind. Whatever is in our hearts comes along with us. When angry people move from old houses, angry people move into new houses. When angry people leave old jobs, angry people enter new jobs.

Moving might be a good time to rid ourselves of excess baggage. Forgiveness is an effective means of jettisoning the weight of anger and bitterness. Forgiving old hurts offers the hope of new beginnings. Remember, our hearts, like our shadows, travel with us wherever we go.

MARCH

Relationships cannot always heal; people can.

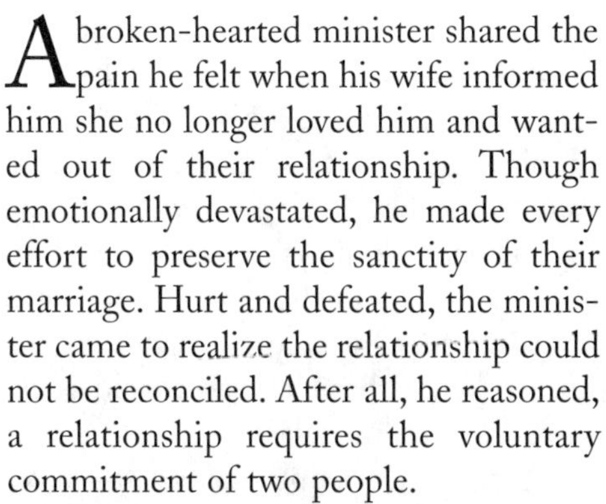

A broken-hearted minister shared the pain he felt when his wife informed him she no longer loved him and wanted out of their relationship. Though emotionally devastated, he made every effort to preserve the sanctity of their marriage. Hurt and defeated, the minister came to realize the relationship could not be reconciled. After all, he reasoned, a relationship requires the voluntary commitment of two people.

For many, post-divorce forgiveness is one of life's most difficult tasks. Broken hopes, dreams, promises, and lives lay in the wake of broken relationships.

Fortunately, forgiveness does not require reconciliation of broken relationships. Rather, forgiveness requires the reconciliation of our own emotional and spiritual resources. While broken relationships cannot always heal, forgiveness offers healing to broken people.

2

People change; donkeys don't, except when people are intent on making donkeys of themselves.

One of the most interesting stories in the Bible is the story of Balaam whose donkey broke the barriers of communication and taught the prophet a valuable lesson. Aside from this intriguing incident, donkeys in the twenty-first century live about the same as they have always lived. On the other hand, life for human beings has changed considerably since the days of Balaam.

Yet, some people refuse to make changes in themselves which would lead to a significantly improved quality of life. At times all of us are like donkeys refusing to give up toxic attitudes and relinquish resentments which inhibit the maturation of our lives. For instance, refusing to forgive others and holding onto spite is a human example of stubbornness often observed in donkeys.

The practice of forgiveness does not make us better than other people; rather, forgiveness liberates us to be more like the person God has in mind for all of us.

The practice of forgiveness can be a long, arduous road, but it is not the road to moral superiority. Most of us deeply admire those who demonstrate magnanimous forgiveness. Yet, most forgiveness takes place in the solitude of broken human hearts.

The practice of forgiveness is courageous and worthy, but it does not make us better than other people. Everyone is given the capacity to forgive others. Not everyone chooses to be forgiving.

The ability to forgive is deeply implanted in the human heart by our Creator. Yet, our Creator forces no one to practice forgiveness. Forgiveness is a choice, but a choice which frees us to be more like the person God had in mind for each of us from our first moments of life.

4

You cain't make a mule to work if he ain't had no oats."

—Folk-saying in West Alabama

Folklore is an important conduit for passing along acquired wisdom. A few grammarians may be offended by the double negatives and miss the intent. But the truth remains: to achieve a result we must make at least some investment.

A bushel of oats may give a mule enough strength to plow a whole field. But the implied wisdom goes far beyond mules, plows, and fields. Investment in strengthening ourselves is a basic tenet of life. Mental, emotional, and spiritual development require nourishment.

In the event we find ourselves harboring anger and resentment toward others, we might consider the likelihood we are spiritually and emotionally undernourished. Forgiveness is wonderful nourishment. It is not necessary to eat an entire bushel unless you feel the need to plow a whole field.

"It's the squeaky wheel that gets the oil."

Sometimes life seems to run smoothly. We find ourselves at peace with ourselves and with the world. These are wonderful times and should be enjoyed to the fullest. Unfortunately, life is not always so serene. Sooner or later we encounter difficulties and life ceases being so smooth. At such times, we may fear our lives are grinding to a halt.

A few squeaks now and then are normal. But squeaks do not generally cure themselves. Squeaks should be considered calls for attention. Some common squeaks which could lead to more serious trouble include: increased irritability, change in appetite, loss of patience, change in sleep habits, and repetitious angry thoughts. Forgiveness is an excellent all-purpose lubrication for squeaky living. Apply liberally. The oil of forgiveness is not in short supply.

6 *"It is not what he has, nor even what he does, which directly expresses the worth of a man, but what he is."*

—Henri Frederic Amiel, *Treasure Chest*

Wealth, position, and influence are often considered social bases for power. Powerful people are generally given respect. Of course, wealth, position, and influence are not assurances one is respectable.

The true worth of a person is a measure of that person's character. Character is independent of wealth, position, or influence. Character is a quality found in the heart. Solomon in his wisdom observed, "…as he thinketh in his heart, so is he."

The Bible tells the story of Stephen, an early disciple. There is no indication Stephen was wealthy or otherwise stalwart. He indeed preached at least one powerful sermon for which he was stoned to death. Yet, it was at the moment of his death his true worth was expressed in the forgiveness of those who took his life.

"Every child comes with the message that God is not yet discouraged of man."

—Rabindranath Tagore

Every child has the right to be welcomed into the world with love and support. Each child is born totally helpless and fully dependent on parents or others for life.

Yet, each child offers the world new hope. Each child is a new opportunity. Each child is born free of heartaches and hatreds. Each child is a new and fresh creation.

The birth of a child is an affirmation that God is willing to entrust the destiny of that child to our hands. We are encouraged to train up a child in the way he or she should go and assured such training will endure.

Children must be taught forgiveness. God is not yet discouraged with us as He continues to forgive each of us. Therefore, let us teach forgiveness even as we are forgiven.

8

"This is what I found out about religion: It gives you courage to make decisions you must make in a crisis and the confidence to leave the results to a higher power."

—Dwight D. Eisenhower

Religion should not be confused with how, when, or even if one practices worship. Worship is often practiced in churches, synagogues, mosques, temples, or even in the privacy of one's closet. On the other hand, religion is the translation of our beliefs into words and deeds. Religion extends beyond the confines of worship.

Religion equips us to take command of our lives. Religion empowers us with moral fortitude and courage to do that which is right even when doing right is met with scorn and disapproval.

The practice of forgiveness is available to everyone. It is not limited to any religious affiliation. Forgiveness is a life force which equips us to withstand attacks, recover, and leave the results to a Higher Power.

"Grant us brotherhood, not only for this day but for all our years—a brotherhood not of words but of acts and deeds."

—Stephen Vincent Benet

Most of us recall learning in grade school to work with fractions. One of the basic skills needed to work with fractions is the ability to find common denominators. Some of us had to relearn this skill when our children struggled with the same homework we did many years ago.

Learning common denominators has more application than adding, subtracting, multiplying, and dividing fractions. There are common denominators which help us understand other people. For instance, other people laugh, cry, hurt, and rejoice. These common denominators help us touch each other and establish a rapport of love and compassion.

The need to forgive and be forgiven are common denominators which should not be overlooked.

10

"The question is not what a man can scorn, or disparage, or find fault with, but what he can love, value, and appreciate."

—John Ruskin

Anyone can criticize. No special talents are required. Fault-finding takes very little practice. Even Michelangelo was not exempt. He had many detractors who failed to appreciate the quality of his work.

A spirit of fault-finding and criticism tends to become chronic. Negative people are predisposed to find other negative people and end up reinforcing each others' negativism. Parents quickly react to the negative behaviors of children and seldom express approval for children who do right.

Forgiveness overcomes the spirit of scorn and criticism. Forgiveness accepts the frailty of human behavior but lays aside condemnation and fault-finding. Forgiveness is built on love, compassion, and appreciation for ourselves and those who share life with us.

"If you have built castles in the air, your work need not be lost; that is where they should be. Now put foundations under them."

—Henry David Thoreau

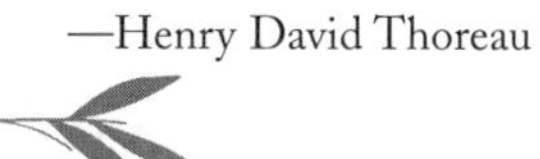

Ideas provide the workshop for creating great accomplishments. Ideas fired by imagination can become cornerstones upon which building blocks transform concepts into reality.

Good intentions begin as good ideas. But good ideas have little value unless they are followed by positive actions. Good ideas are like air castles without foundations. Putting a good idea into practice is to provide the foundation of reality.

Forgiveness is a noble idea. It is a beautiful concept readily fired by our imaginations. But forgiveness is only an air castle until it is set on a solid foundation. That foundation is set into place the moment we erase the debt of someone who has hurt us.

12 *"Real joy comes not from ease or riches or from the praise of men, but from doing something worthwhile."*

—Wilfred T. Grenfell

Most of us have very little impact on the world around us. Fame and fortune are generally directed toward a powerful minority. Yet, does that mean we are not worthwhile?

Regardless of circumstances or our station in life, each of us has opportunities to make our world a better place. The greatest of all treasure is human life. To become a better person, to lift others in need, to forgive when offended, is to make our world a better place.

Forgiving people may not necessarily enjoy riches or the praise of others. But forgiving people know the real joy of doing something worthwhile. True "worthwhileness" lifts others. Jesus summarized this truth when He taught, "Inasmuch as ye have done it unto one of the least of these my brethren, ye have done it unto me."

"Earth's crammed with heaven, and every common bush afire with God."
—Elizabeth Barrett Browning

The world often appears to be a hostile, frightening environment. Wars and rumors of wars have always been disturbing. Human capacity for inhumanity is a harsh reality which may overshadow the beauty of God's creation.

Forgiveness offers a means of overcoming human hatred. Forgiveness is realistic. Rather than gloss over the ugliness of human behavior, forgiveness confronts the worst in human nature. Yet, forgiveness opens the way to inner peace and reconciliation.

We may not be able to control world events or even the spiteful behavior of those in our own neighborhoods. Yet, by practicing the art of forgiveness, our eyes may envision the peace of heaven on earth and presence of God among imperfect human beings.

14

"Be angry, but do not sin."

—Ephesians 4:26

When we are attacked or offended, our first reaction is anger. It's only natural. But we've all learned we can't always act on every natural urge—not even anger. And sometimes we learn this the hard way. We need to take the time to choose or decide what to do with our anger. Like a laser, anger can be a potent force for destruction—or for healing. Anger misused can destroy relationships; used effectively, anger can cut surgically through emotional debris. Allowing healing change to happen.

"The best cosmetic in the world is an active mind that is always finding something new."

—Mary Meek Atkeson

Cosmetic surgery is growing in popularity. Hair transplants and "tummy tucks" are fairly common. There is some evidence indicating our appearance tends to affect our personalities and how others respond to us.

Yet, the truth remains, one's image is not a reliable indicator of the quality of one's soul. To be sure, appearance is important. For instance angry people often wear clinched expressions. Worried people may have deeply furrowed brows; content people smile easily.

Forgiveness has a wonderful way of softening facial lines. Forgiveness offers a durable beauty allowing us to age gracefully. Forgiveness is more than a cosmetic process. By ridding us of acrid feelings of anger and hurt, forgiveness actually changes the soul.

16

"I have no yesterdays, time took them away; Tomorrow may not be—but I have today."

—Pearl Yeadon McGinnis

We often say to one another, "Have a nice day!" We wish each other a nice day as a cheerful blessing. We are optimistic about today because the day at hand is our opportunity to make life good for ourselves and others.

We would never say to our friends, "Have a nice yesterday." Such an expression would be ridiculous, as yesterday has been recorded in history and cannot be changed. Yet, unresolved conflicts from yesterday can pollute opportunities for today and hopes for a brighter future.

While forgiveness sorts out conflicts from our past, today is our opportunity to forgive those who created those conflicts. Forgiveness today assures a better tomorrow. Have a nice day!

Forgiving the Dead

A middle-aged lady lamented, "I'm finally able to forgive my father, but it is too late! He died last year." Sometimes we mistakenly assume we cannot forgive those who have passed on.

To be sure, we often feel controlled from beyond the grave by those who may have cruelly mistreated us. We may illogically conjecture they cannot rest in peace as long as hatred for them continues to live in our hearts. In bitterness, we may feel justified. After all, why should they rest in peace while we are continually tormented? Fortunately, this middle-aged lady discovered dead people can and should be forgiven. Forgiveness takes place in our hearts and requires nothing from those who have violated us.

May our hearts rest in peace while we yet live.

18

Put justice into the hands of the law; put forgiveness into the depths of your heart.

Victims and their families often look to the judicial system for justice. A common objective is to find "closure." Many indicate they cannot experience closure until justice has been served and appropriate punishment has been meted out to the offender.

Unfortunately, closure on this basis is often elusive.

Forgiveness is more than closure. Closure only signifies the conclusion of legal procedures. Forgiveness is more than closure; it is resolution. Forgiveness does not take place in a court. Forgiveness takes place in our hearts. Closure is not dependable. Forgiveness is as dependable as our willingness to put it into practice.

"Forgiveness does not mean accepting further abuse or continuing destructive relationships. Establish boundaries for what is acceptable to you and make these boundaries clear to others. Hold them accountable for their actions."

—Forgiveness Therapy

Forgiveness does not mean we volunteer to become someone's doormat. Forgiveness does not mean we approve of another's misbehavior. Forgiveness does not mean we refrain from protecting ourselves from further abuse. Forgiveness does not mean we allow ourselves to continue in abusive relationships. Forgiveness does not mean offenders are not accountable.

We have a right to justice. However, holding others responsible should never be done in malice or as a vendetta. Serious offenders need to be held accountable. Some perpetrators are violent and need to be incarcerated for the protection of ourselves and everyone else. Establishing boundaries and making those boundaries clear is an indication of healthy self-esteem. We need not hate to be firm.

20

"Sometimes people hurt you because, like you, they are learning and growing. Forgive their incompleteness, their humanness."

—Forgiveness Therapy

A man once complimented a lady's new hairstyle. The lady immediately broke into tears. She accused the man of ridiculing her. Through tears she sobbed how much she hated her new hairstyle and could not understand how anyone could find it attractive.

As we might anticipate, the man felt terrible. His compliment had been sincere. He would never intentionally inflict such pain on anyone. Fortunately, the lady forgave him.

Most of us have been in similar situations. Perhaps we have all experienced the relief of being forgiven for our unintentional behavior.

Of course, sooner or later someone will unintentionally hurt us. This is an unavoidable part of being and living among people. When we experience these hurts, remember what it was like to be forgiven.

"Confront those who have hurt you; tell them how you feel. When that is impossible or when that could harm you or someone else, speak to them in your imagination."

—Forgiveness Therapy

Confronting others should not be confused with angry accusations. Confrontation is not to hurt others as they have hurt us; rather, confrontation is for clarification. Confrontation clears the air.

Effective confrontation is concise. It is not for the purpose of dredging up old offenses. Confrontation should never be used as a means to spew forth pent-up bitterness. Confrontation simply delineates the offense for both the victim and the offender.

Direct confrontation is often helpful but not essential. For instance, a thirty-five-year-old lady chose not to tell her family about a now deceased uncle who abused her many years ago. Telling her family would only hurt them. Instead, she confronted her uncle in the privacy of her forgiving meditations. In those quiet moments, healing took place.

22

"To refuse to forgive is to continue to hurt yourself. Victimized once, your lack of forgiveness keeps you stuck as a victim, holding on to a victim's identity. Instead, claim the identity of one who forgives."

—Forgiveness Therapy

Victimization hurts! Most victims need emotional support and understanding. While emotional support and understanding are comforting, they are not necessarily healing.

Being healed is even more important. The role of victim should be temporary. Comfort equips us to move on to healing. Healing comes through forgiveness.

Victims usually cannot help being victimized. However, victims can choose to forgive and heal. To delay moving on to forgiveness and healing is like being victimized a second time. While we could not help the first victimization, indeed the second victimization is within our control. We did not deserve being victimized the first time. We certainly do not deserve victimizing ourselves by refusing to forgive and heal.

"If you find it hard to forgive your parents for their imperfect parenting, remember: They were shaped by the imperfect parenting they received from parents who were shaped by their own parenting, and so on and so on…"

—Forgiveness Therapy

All parents make mistakes and these mistakes are not limited to minor flaws in our parenting skills. Unfortunately, most people are not prepared for parenthood. Most of our parenting skills were learned from parents who were no more prepared for parenting than ourselves.

An older family therapist once commented he had worked with members of extended families who had carried anger, bitterness, and dysfunction into four generations. Angry, unforgiving parents have a strong tendency to raise angry, unforgiving children.

Each new generation represents new hope. Imagine, the idea of forgiving our parents may be the beginning of breaking that cycle in our own family. Teaching our children the art of forgiveness may endow them with a heritage which will live for generations to come.

24

"Know that forgiveness is possible even when someone doesn't seem to deserve forgiveness. It is a testimony to the goodness your Creator instilled within you from the first moment of your being."

—Forgiveness Therapy

Forgiveness is always possible unless we make it impossible. We tend to limit the scope of forgiveness to forgiving only those worthy of our trust and respect. After all, nice people who make mistakes are reasonably easy to forgive.

But what about those who do not merit our trust or respect? What about those who do not want our forgiveness? What about those who will continue hurting us whether we forgive them or not? Are such people forgivable? Yes, but only if we dig deeper into the wellsprings of our souls.

Fortunately, our Creator has instilled in each of us the capacity to forgive unlovely people under adverse circumstances. Sometimes this capability gets lost. Yet, the love of our Creator graciously reaffirms our ability to forgive, even when forgiveness seems impossible.

Seven-year-old Walter's mother directed, "It is time to clean up your room." Walter ignored the order; his mother repeated her command—this time with firmness. Hearing sternness, Walter asserted, "I don't want to!" Walter's mother responded, *"Do it anyway!"* Most of us can sympathize with Walter. None of us enjoys cleaning up a mess. Walter did not understand he had to live in his room and someday he alone would be responsible for cleaning it up.

For many of us, forgiving others can be compared to Walter's feelings. Failing to forgive others means we live in our own messy rooms.

Whenever you hear yourself say, "I don't want to forgive," take charge of your life, practice self-discipline and *do it anyway!*

26

"Forgiveness is the only real prescription for the pain you feel over someone else's behavior. The healing choice is yours to make."

—Forgiveness Therapy

Since forgiveness is such an effective prescription for the agony produced by the misbehavior of others, why is forgiveness so commonly overlooked? Possibly, because anger requires no effort; forgiveness can test the depths of our souls. Initially, anger offers the illusion of regaining our emotional equilibrium. We may allow our feelings to rage out of control. Once these feelings have been exhausted, we hope to return to some semblance of sanity. Unfortunately, exhausted rage is only resting. These feelings can resuscitate unexpectedly. Forgiveness is realistic but also provides release for pent-up angry feelings. Forgiveness declares rage null and void. The dregs are swept from our hearts.

Anger happens because we *let* it happen. Forgiveness happens because we *make* it happen. The healing choice is ours.

"When someone won't forgive you, refusing to forgive in return is no answer. That's like wrapping yourself in the other's chains. Keep yourself free; forgive."

—Forgiveness Therapy

Forgiveness can never be forced. No one can force anyone to forgive them. Neither can anyone force us to forgive someone else. Forgiveness is always voluntary; it is always a matter of choice.

Forgiving those who refuse to forgive us seems more difficult. After all, those who refuse to forgive us are in no position to appreciate our forgiveness.

One forgiving person should be enough. Refusing to forgive someone who will not forgive us makes two unforgiving people. Two unforgiving people are not likely to find resolution or reconciliation.

Instead, be patient with those who either cannot forgive us or fail to reciprocate our forgiveness. Recall a time when forgiveness seemed impossible. By freeing ourselves from their chains, we may also show them the way to freedom.

28 *The very idea of forgiveness can make us angry.*

Sometimes the very idea of forgiveness strikes us as shallow. Smarting from an inflicted injury, we may find ourselves resenting the idea of forgiveness. Furthermore, we may resent anyone who would suggest such a seemingly inane idea.

After all, when someone mistreats us we have a right to be angry. The idea of forgiveness may seem to erode what few rights we have left. We might rationalize that anyone who recommends forgiveness does not appreciate how much we hurt. Ironically, we not only find ourselves angry at the offender, we may also become angry at those who counsel forgiveness. Such anger seems to compound itself.

Yet in truth, the more angered we become at the idea of forgiveness, the more forgiveness is needed.

Self-forgiveness requires a conscience.

A boy in early adolescence got involved with a gang of violent teenagers. Eager to prove himself, he robbed a convenience store. During the robbery he shot a store clerk in the back of the head. Miraculously, the clerk survived. Due to his age, the boy was given probation and returned to his mother. In his mind he dismissed the robbery and shooting as inconsequential.

Yet, deep in his heart the boy was troubled. His grades dropped. His home life was difficult. Finally his probation officer referred him for counseling.

Slowly, the young man began to understand the pain he had inflicted on the man and his family. Overwhelmed, his heart was broken. A healthy conscience replaced his hardened heart. Self-forgiveness changed the course of his life.

30 *When it seems your suffering will never end...*

Is forgiveness possible when there is no end to suffering? Some forms of victimization leave permanent disabilities and indelible emotional scars. For instance, a violent attacker may leave us permanently crippled. A murderer may leave us devastated with grief by taking the life of a loved one. Such damage is beyond repair.

Forgiveness is very difficult when we must cope with the damage of someone else's criminal behavior for the rest of our lives. Forgiveness may be even more difficult when the perpetrator is free to live a normal life.

In truth, forgiveness takes place in our hearts and is possible as long as we have life. Not only is forgiveness possible when our suffering will never end, it may be our only chance for true wholeness.

No one deserves forgiveness; that is why it is called forgiveness.

Like ourselves, other people have power and the ability to choose how they will use their power. Sometimes they choose to use their power to injure us or hurt us emotionally. These choices may be very intentional and designed to inflict upon us maximum damage.

Such willful acts are hard to forgive. Our first reaction may be to declare these people do not merit forgiveness. Indeed this is true. But then we are all guilty of intentionally hurting others and are no more deserving of forgiveness than anyone else.

In reality, if forgiveness were warranted, there would be no need to forgive. Forgiveness is the power to restore ourselves from damage maliciously inflicted upon us by undeserving people. Forgive those who despitefully use you; you deserve it.

April

"Forget about forgetting an injury. That's not always possible—and maybe at times not always desirable. Rather, choose to move on, past remembering to forgiveness."

—Forgiveness Therapy

Forgetting about an injury may not be possible. Some neurologists tell us memories are indelibly hard-wired into brain circuits. Yet, remember an injury is not the same as an obsession with having been hurt by someone else's spiteful behavior.

If brain circuitry cannot be deleted, can it at least be changed? Probably so. Pioneering research indicates brain chemistry and structure can actually be changed by changing the way we think. Such changes affect how we feel. What a fascinating discovery!

Consider what changes may actually occur in our brains if we think more about forgiveness and less about hate. What if we became obsessed with love and forgiveness? No doubt the practice of forgiveness is an adventure into the frontiers of human development with many fascinating discoveries.

2

"Let forgiveness be the catalyst for a healthy chain reaction. Forgiveness sterilizes the wound, which permits healing, which releases energy for growth."

—Forgiveness Therapy

The longer we hold on to unresolved bitterness and anger, the more potent these toxins of the soul become. Spiritual and emotional infections can become unmanageable; the results are devastating.

New viral and bacterial strains are constantly evolving which are resistant to known medications. For example, a young girl with a terminal disease was taken off her medications. Her doctor hoped to prevent an immunity so her medications would be effective as her disease progresses.

There is no risk of developing an immunity to forgiveness. There is certainly no risk of overdosing. All side effects are positive. Forgiveness overcomes spiritual and emotional toxins which deplete our strength. Forgiveness releases energy for dynamic living.

"No loving relationship is free of hurts. Bind up the wounds of love with forgiveness."

—Forgiveness Therapy

Any human relationship that is free of hurts is not really a relationship. Whenever and wherever human beings interact, differences occur, and feelings get hurt. Wounds are particularly excruciating when inflicted by someone we love. As many as half of all marriages end in divorce. Obviously, the practice of forgiveness in loving relationships seems to be in short supply.

Forgiveness is no assurance broken relationships can or should be reconciled. However, healthy reconciliation is practically impossible without forgiveness.

Relationships are one of the great treasures of life. Yet relationships, like people, can be hurt and damaged by thoughtless or malicious behavior. Forgiveness is a healing balm. Every loving relationship requires liberal applications.

4

"Forgiveness may seem futile when you see no immediate results. But healing and growth are like fine, aged cheese—not instant masked potatoes. Give forgiveness time."

—Forgiveness Therapy

A few years ago computers seemed miraculous. Now computers must also be fast. Each new generation of technology is superseded in a few months by faster and more powerful micro-chips.

In an age of micro-chips we have become impatient waiting for anything. We have become accustomed to instant results.

Unfortunately, the art of forgiveness has not caught up with modern technology. The human heart still heals at the same rate; a rate which at times seems impossibly slow.

Keep in mind forgiveness changes only our own hearts, but those changes are profound and worth whatever time is required.

"No offense is unforgivable—unless you make it so. Use your power wisely."
—Forgiveness Therapy

Where are the boundaries between what is forgivable and what is not forgivable? Indeed, this is a complex rhetorical question. Yet, the answer is simple. Those boundaries are set within our own hearts.

Fortunately, the boundaries between what is forgivable and what is not forgivable are movable. Since those boundaries are set within our hearts, we may re-survey and move them at will. Whenever we encounter an unforgivable circumstance, we are free to enlarge our own boundaries.

The power of forgiveness is not limited to the magnitude of the offense. The power of forgiveness is only limited by the boundaries we draw for ourselves. Claim as much territory as you need. Indeed, no offense is unforgivable—unless you make it so. Use your power wisely.

6 *"Forgiveness is a lifelong process. Forgive over and over—even for the same offense."*

—Forgiveness Therapy

Forgiving an offense does not necessarily qualify us as a forgiving person. Forgiving an offense, especially a major one, is a good start and at least we are moving in the right direction.

Forgiving one's father does not mean one has forgiven his or her mother. Forgiving one's spouse does not mean one has forgiven his or her boss. Each situation represents a separate issue and requires a separate act of forgiveness. Yet, each act of forgiveness helps strengthen us into becoming more forgiving people. Mothers, fathers, spouses, bosses, friends, along with ourselves, are just a few of the important people in our lives who require ongoing forgiveness. Practice does not make perfect, but people who stay in practice find ongoing forgiveness much less difficult.

"Forgiveness is not something you do for someone else; it is something you do for yourself. Give yourself the gift of forgiveness."

—Forgiveness Therapy

When someone forgives us we generally feel better. Therefore, we might assume when we forgive others, we are doing them a favor. Indeed, the person we forgive may feel better and even express appreciation for our forgiveness.

On the other hand, we may assume withholding our forgiveness will guarantee the offender will feel bad. We may erroneously reason, as long as we feel bad, they should feel bad too.

Withholding forgiveness only assures we will continue to harbor anger within ourselves. Forgiveness is a gift we give ourselves. To forgive others is to give ourselves better feelings, restored dignity, and a sense of inner peace. We may be assured forgiveness is working when we hope offenders feel better too.

I remember when...

Memories are often associated with important events and important events are often associated with memories. Important memories often associate events and dates. Birthdays, anniversaries, graduations, and deaths are a few important events which change the course of our lives.

Connecting important decisions to dates and events is one reason many of us make New Year's resolutions. One grandfather stopped smoking when his first grandchild was born. On her sixteenth birthday they both enjoyed a special celebration.

Determining to forgive a major hurt is an important event. Mark that event in time. Associating such forgiveness with a new year, a new commitment to life, or perhaps a new job, will remind us to celebrate the freedom of forgiveness long after we have overcome our anger.

"To help you forgive, picture the other person surrounded by the light of God. See yourself stepping into that light, and feel God's presence with you both."

—Forgiveness Therapy

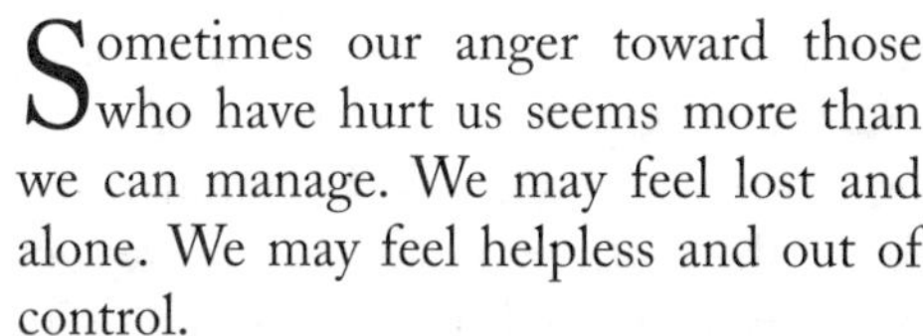

Sometimes our anger toward those who have hurt us seems more than we can manage. We may feel lost and alone. We may feel helpless and out of control.

When there is no love or forgiveness left in our souls, our only resources are spiritual. We may have no viable alternative to looking beyond ourselves to a power greater than ourselves.

Yet, spiritual resources may seem impossibly distant when we are angry. When we experience hate, love seems so far away.

One beautiful way to connect ourselves with spiritual resources available to all of us is to envision the offender stepping into the warm light of God's immeasurable love. In prayerful meditation step into that light and forgive even as you too are forgiven.

10

"Recognize how you've refused to forgive. Keeping inner monsters at bay requires energy. Instead, use your energy to affirm and embrace life."

—Forgiveness Therapy

Children seem to have an abundance of energy. Most parents find their energy has limitations. Children often wear their parents down. As we get older, most of us learn to use our finite energy judiciously.

Energy should be used, not wasted. Living in anger and refusing to forgive exacts a heavy toll on our spiritual and emotional stamina. Lacking energy, we may lose our zest for life.

Anger, hate, and hurt create unpredictable monsters within our souls. We may find ourselves like wild animal trainers expending most of our energy attempting to control our savage feelings. Forgiveness frees this energy for more productive living. Use your new energy wisely.

"Victims are helpless, at the mercy of the offender. By showing mercy to an offender, you put yourself back in control. Take control by forgiving."

—Forgiveness Therapy

Grace is commonly defined as unmerited favor. Grace is among the most beautiful of all characteristics. Like forgiveness, grace is taught and modeled by our Creator.

Sometimes offenders hurt too. Offenders may find themselves overwhelmed with guilt for having hurt us. They may feel a sense of shame and loss of personal dignity. In short, they may experience the same feelings we have felt when we have been guilty of hurting someone else.

Those who violate us may or may not show mercy. Yet, we may always choose to extend to them the grace of forgiveness tempered with mercy. By recalling times when we have hurt others, we may experience compassion for those who have hurt us. As with forgiveness, mercy is not only to be received, it is a grace to be freely given.

12

"If you withhold forgiveness until a wrong is made right, you risk condemning yourself to a life sentence of bitterness; you risk letting your life be shaped by someone else's actions."

—Forgiveness Therapy

Newton's third law of motion stipulates, "For every action force there is an equal and opposite reaction force."

However, forgiveness is seldom balanced with consistent laws. In fact the rules for effective forgiveness often seem out of balance. For instance, forgiveness does not require an apology or restitution unless we choose to impose them as prerequisites.

Of course, we may impose any qualifications we choose as conditions for our forgiveness. Yet, to do so is at our own peril. Those who willfully violate us may not care about our feelings or even consider an apology. Sometimes, restitution is impossible. We have then condemned ourselves to life behind bars of our own making.

Apologies are good. Restitution is better. Forgiveness is best.

"Don't put conditions on your forgiveness, or your inner peace will depend on the decision of the person who hurt you."

—Forgiveness Therapy

Risk is a part of life, but may not be a part of forgiveness. Putting conditions on forgiveness works sometimes but is risky. We may require an apology. Should the offender apologize and we forgive, our inner peace may be restored.

However, the offender may not apologize. In that event, wc remain disturbed. We have put our own inner peace at risk by putting control into the hands of one who has hurt us and does not care enough to apologize. Our last state may be worse than our original pain.

Putting conditions on our forgiveness is not acceptable. We are more likely to make better choices concerning our inner peace than remorseless adversaries.

14

"Allow forgiveness to open the door to reconciliation. Today's bully could be tomorrow's friend."

—Forgiveness Therapy

Forgiveness is not reconciliation. Forgiveness simply makes reconciliation possible.

Yet, reconciliation can be very rewarding and should not be overlooked. Anger and resentment invariably affect our view of offenders. At best, we may think of them as thoughtless and inconsiderate. Most of the time our evaluation is much more severe.

Forgiveness affords us the opportunity to reevaluate those who have hurt us. By resolving hurt and animosity in our hearts, an offender may appear differently. At least we begin viewing them as human beings. We might also begin to appreciate character qualities which had been previously eclipsed by our anger.

Sometimes the rewards of forgiveness are unexpected. Perhaps when we least expect it, we might even find a new friend.

"Accept the possibility of rebuilding a relationship. Past offenses can be bull-dozed and buried and a better life built atop the debris."

—Forgiveness Therapy

15 APRIL

Refusing to forgive destroys many good relationships. In such cases everyone loses. We should never assume a relationship should end simply because mistakes have been made. In some cases forgiveness can even strengthen a relationship.

Offenses must be completely buried to realistically reconstruct a relationship. Unfortunately, some prefer to "bury the hatchet" but are careful to "leave the handle out" just in case.

Archeologists often find mounds where one city has been built on top of another. City after city might be totally destroyed, leveled out and a new city built atop the debris.

Relationships can be restored in a similar fashion. Even though a relationship lays in ruins, consider bulldozing anger and hurt.

16 *When Trust Is Broken*

Trust can be confused with many qualities of human relationships. Commonly, love and trust are muddled. Certainly love is enhanced by trust in a loving relationship. However, we may love people we do not trust and trust people we do not love. For instance, we might not love our banker, but we trust him or her with our paychecks.

Neither love nor forgiveness are contingent on trust. Forgiveness and trust must not be enmeshed. We may forgive but trust is not necessarily restored. Yet, both love and forgiveness are enhanced when trust is also a part of the relationship. We grow to forgive the unforgivable. But only a fool trusts the untrustworthy. When trust is broken, trust must be rebuilt. Forgiveness clears our emotional roadblocks which would impede the rebuilding of trust.

Rebuilding Broken Trust in a Loving Relationship

Sometimes trust cannot be restored simply because the person who has violated trust refuses to be trustworthy. However, people who do not merit trust can and should be forgiven. Forgiveness clears our own obstacles. Without forgiveness, trust may be nearly impossible to reestablish. To rebuild trust, set the foundation on forgiveness.

Forgiveness requires nothing of the offender. However, rebuilding trust requires trustworthy behavior. This is an important distinction. Sometimes when the perpetrator cannot be trusted, we might falsely assume we have failed to adequately forgive that person.

Rebuilding trust must begin with forgiveness. Become hyper-vigilant for small areas of trust. Build trust slowly by offering opportunities for trust.

18 *You can't teach an old dog new tricks.*

Are we ever too old to learn? Depends. Sometimes even young people allow their minds to shut down. On the other hand, some elderly people stay active by learning and developing new skills. One student pilot in Ohio is 100 years old and flies without medical restrictions.

Are we ever too old to forgive? Are injuries and hurts ever too old to heal? Only if we shut our hearts and let our spiritual selves atrophy. Age may deteriorate the body but need not deteriorate the soul.

Deathbed forgiveness is an effort to hold on to bitterness until the very last. Such forgiveness has dubious value. One may indeed forgive in the last moments of life, but this is to rob oneself of a lifetime of healing and growth.

"I see people as trees, walking."

Jesus once gave sight to a blind man then asked the man what he saw. The man replied, "I see people as trees, walking." At first the man's response seems very strange. Yet, our own perceptions are often inaccurate and misleading. Revenge may seem sweet; forgiveness a weakness.

A common perceptual problem is known as dyslexia. Words and letters appear reversed, which of course is confusing and makes learning difficult for afflicted persons.

Yet, a more common problem might be thought of as spiritual or emotional dyslexia. Instead of a *learning* disability, this may be considered a *living* disability.

Forgiveness helps put the world into proper perspective. Jesus once again touched the man, "...and he was restored, and saw every man clearly."

20 *"No one can make you feel bad. You have the power to choose between getting bitter and getting better."*

Why do some people become easily angered while others do not? Some individuals are willing to maim or kill over name-calling or slurs. Others are impervious to the same attacks.

Of course those who are unaffected are confident in themselves and take responsibility for their own feelings. With responsibility comes the power of choice. With the power of choice comes self-control. With self-control comes personal confidence.

No one can make us feel bad unless we allow them to do so. Certainly if we choose to feel bad, we can choose not to feel bad.

Forgiveness is also a choice. If we choose not to forgive, we also have the power to choose forgiveness. With renewed self-confidence, claim your power.

"You cannot change someone for the better by holding a grudge. Grudges change only you—for the worse."

—Forgiveness Therapy

Most magicians acknowledge they do not really have the power of magic. They provide fascinating entertainment by convincing us what we see is not what really happens.

Holding a grudge is one of life's great illusions. Somehow by holding a grudge we hope to find peace by evening the score against those who have hurt us. Yet, when we inflict pain on others, the illusion of peace vanishes and leaves us feeling shame.

Holding a grudge may offer the illusionary hope of changing the offender. In reality, grudges tend to make offenders even more antagonistic.

A grudge allows anger to become embedded in our hearts. Forgiveness is not magic, nor is it illusionary. But we might be amazed at the changes forgiveness can make in our lives.

22 *Limited Lifetime Warranty*

What does Limited Lifetime Warranty really mean? What is actually covered? Whose lifetime? The lifetime of the purchaser? The product? The company who made the product? Or perhaps the lifetime of the paper on which the warranty is printed.

Of course reputable manufacturers may go beyond the limits specified in the warranty. Established companies know the importance of satisfied customers.

Sometimes we may offer only a limited lifetime warranty on our forgiveness. This simply means we extend forgiveness, but leave enough loopholes to rescind our forgiveness at will.

Reputable firms know the value of happy customers. Should our forgiveness be any different?

A Walk in the Garden

Sometimes the task of forgiving seems overwhelming. Human beings are capable of indescribable atrocities. We may seriously question if forgiveness can be stretched to cover the full gamut of human transgression.

Such questions remain academic until we are personally affected. When we, or someone we love, are the victims of such outrageous assaults we might wonder if our souls can survive the struggle. A few might even prefer to die.

When forgiveness seems beyond hope, take an evening walk in the garden. Let the cool breeze soothe the rage in your soul. Enjoy the fragrance. Perhaps pray until you are exhausted.

Listen carefully and you will find the strength and courage to forgive. For in those moments you have walked in Gethsemane.

24 *Don't beat a dead horse.*

Angry people have a tendency to serve endless portions of rehashed leftovers. Old offenses lay just beneath the surface ready to pounce at the slightest provocation.

Some families use holidays as occasions to celebrate old conflicts. Reminders of previous offenses are exchanged like old Christmas cards.

Somehow the details of old dissensions get worse with each recitation. Minor differences stretch into horrendous disagreements. Old conflicts never die; they don't even fade away.

Beating a dead horse is an indication genuine forgiveness has not taken place. Recalling old offenses is a testimony to an unforgiving spirit.

Eight-year-old Nancy who had never heard the idiom, "beating a dead horse," asked, "Isn't that kinda stupid?" Yes, Nancy, you are exactly right.

"Ask yourself whether 'I can't forgive' means 'I won't forgive.' Then turn your heart toward the warmth of God's love and allow that love to thaw your heart."

—Forgiveness Therapy

The fact we have been victimized does not mean our hearts are pure. In reality our hearts may have become hardened with outraged indignation. As victims we hope for compassion, but we should also examine ourselves for residual bitterness.

To be justifiably angry does not prevent anger from eroding the quality of our character. Our hearts are not exempt from resentment because we have been mistreated.

When angry, "I won't forgive" easily becomes "I can't forgive." We may lose confidence in ourselves; in our ability to cope with unprovoked attacks. We may lose courage and go down in defeat.

The warmth of God's sun brings new life every spring. Certainly, the warmth of His love will thaw our frozen hearts and bring new life to our souls.

26 *"Love covers a multitude of sins—especially mine."*

Sin is an interesting subject until it becomes personal. Forgiveness is intriguing as long as someone else is required to do the forgiving. Self-forgiveness may be one of the most loving expressions we can give ourselves. To be meaningful, love and forgiveness must be personal. The fact love covers a multitude of sins is a beautiful concept. But love becomes more than a beautiful concept when it is applied to our *personal* sins. Of course, personalization of sin and forgiveness causes us to feel uncomfortable. No one enjoys being confronted with unforgiven internal bitterness.

Yet, the doorway to inner comfort and peace is personalization of love and forgiveness. To experience love and forgiveness inspires us to love and forgive in a very personal way.

"Thank God every morning when you get up that you have something to do which must be done, whether you like it or not."

—Charles Kingsley

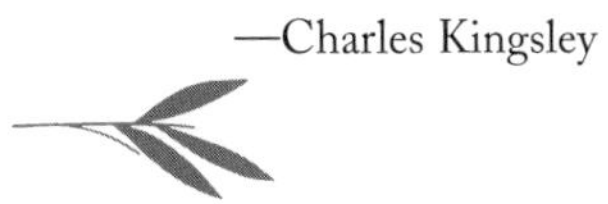

Many people wake up to jobs they do not like. Many feel trapped by financial obligations or other responsibilities. Chained to jobs or lives that are unfulfilling, many greet the day with a sense of dread.

Angry people not only dread their work, their unhappiness is compounded by lethargy or acrid hostility. Such unhappiness also affects our interactions with those around us. Waking up in anger is a sign forgiveness should be on the agenda.

Forgiveness does not guarantee a new job, but rather a new outlook on an old job. Even jobs we do not like have opportunities. Every workplace needs more forgiving people. Forgiving people are worth more and should be paid more. But don't count on it.

"You never miss the water till the well runs dry."

Most of us have tried to turn on a light switch during a power outage. During an extended power outage, we become acutely aware how dependent we are on electricity.

Sometimes, when we have been deeply hurt by someone else, it seems like we are disconnected from life. We may feel lethargic or depressed. We might even lose interest in social interactions. Damaged and hurt, we feel isolated and alone.

To allow ourselves to become disconnected from our spiritual resources is to experience a major power outage. When the lines are down, we lose vitality. We feel helpless and crushed.

By forgiving those who have hurt us, we begin reconnecting with life. Spiritual strength begins to flow into our weakened souls. Once again the healing flow of forgiveness fills our reservoirs.

"All's well that ends well."

Shakespeare wrote, "All the world is a stage." Most of us feel we have little influence on the script. Sometimes we may wonder if we are living or being controlled by life. Even the very purpose of life may seem obscure. Prophets, philosophers, doomsayers, and scientists all have different opinions on wherc we are going and how we will get there.

Yet, our destiny is not completely out of our control. Forgiveness allows us to rewrite many otherwise tragic scenes. Anger, hate, and hostility can be rewritten into love, compassion, and caring. Broken hearts and discouragement can lead to victorious strength.

Most of us have little impact on the destiny of our planet or life as we know it. But each of us is capable of love and forgiveness which gives us the assurance that indeed, all is well that ends well.

Many hurts and injuries which occur in childhood are carried into adult life. When frustrated, children may act like little tyrants. Against all odds, recalcitrant children may contest parental authority and often win.

One common mechanism used by undisciplined children is the use of temper tantrums. These children become focused on their immediate frustrations and rage until they achieve gratification. Unfortunately, many of these children become adults without changing their behavior. As grownups, they now have adult powers. They become spoiled brats in big bodies. Expressions of rage become more serious and destructive.

Forgiveness voids rage and frustration. When one is able to forgive, a legitimate self-respect emerges.

MAY

Crucible of Confusion

Human feelings are often crushed and mixed in an emotional crucible. At times, we may not be sure what emotion we are experiencing. For instance, anger and depression can be confused. Experts tell us we can suffer agitated depression. They also tell us we can hold two opposite feelings at the same time. They call this ambivalence.

Sometimes, anger seems to evolve into hurt. At other times, hurt evolves into anger. As our feelings change, we may feel even more confused. We may find ourselves laughing to keep from crying, or crying to keep from lashing out.

Forgiveness heals a range of confused feelings. Forgiveness instills hope when our hearts are broken. Forgiveness instills courage when we feel defeated. Forgiveness instills love when hate has taken over.

2 *"It is well to think well; it is divine to act well."*

—Horace Mann

Sometimes prayers seem unanswered simply because we have overlooked the obvious. For instance, we might pray, "Give us this day our daily bread." Yet, we have been given the strength and opportunity to earn bread for ourselves and others who may not have our strength or opportunity.

Thinking, loving, and forgiving are intangible. Like answers to prayer, these concepts must be translated into tangible human behavior to have real meaning. Loving people are forgiving people.

There are no set behaviors which define love and forgiveness. Yet, loving and forgiving people are easily recognizable. Our Creator has empowered each of us with creativity and the strength needed to express love and forgiveness. Don't waste too much time praying for something you already have.

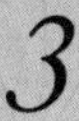

"Forgive. People will wonder what you're up to."

M
A
Y

Forgiveness is probably not normal. At least forgiveness is not usually our first reaction to being mistreated. Our immediate impulse is to retaliate.

Normal reactions are not always healthy reactions. For instance, our normal reflex to strike back at others runs counter to the rules of civilized living.

Forgiveness seems to run contrary to our normal reactions. Forgiveness may even be abnormal. Yet, forgiveness helps us regain our emotional and spiritual balance. Forgiveness allows us to return to normal. Emotional control, peace and tranquility are restored.

Paradoxically, we may have to practice abnormal forgiveness in order to be normal human beings. Forgiveness is just abnormal enough, people will wonder what you are up to.

4 *"Be not angry that you cannot make others as you wish them to be, since you cannot make yourself as you wish to be."*

—Thomas a 'Kempis

One parent summed it up this way: "As a father of two teenagers and one pre-teen, I've had my share of experiences with slammed doors, ugly threats, loud shouts, pouting spells, and angry outbursts. Sometimes my children and wife have even joined me in these activities!"

Anger has a way of pulling everyone into it. But the good news is that we can work together to pull ourselves out of it.

Coals of Fire on Their Heads

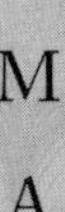

M
A
Y

Forgiveness sounds like a righteous act and indeed true forgiveness is a divine characteristic which can be practiced by human beings. Similarly, love is of God, but human beings can practice love and be loving.

Unfortunately, human expressions of love and forgiveness can be distorted and actually become expressions of evil human traits.

Occasionally, we might find ourselves forgiving our enemies in anticipation of "coals of fire" being heaped on their heads. Insidiously, we may reason, if we cannot effect justice, certainly God will cruelly punish them for us.

We might do well to remember God's love and forgiveness are pure. To pray for the inner peace and tranquility of our enemies is consistent with the divine love and forgiveness God extends to each of us.

6

"How great is the contrast between that forgiveness to which we lay claim from God towards us, and our temper toward others!"

—H. Thornton

Forgiveness is a skill; an art which requires a lifetime of practice. About the time we think we may have mastered the art of forgiveness a new and perhaps more serious offense occurs requiring us to reach deeper into our souls. No doubt, in the course of human life there is no end to honing the skill of forgiveness. At times we may be tempted to abandon our pursuit and allow bitterness to creep into our lives.

At such times, we may regain strength and determination by reminding ourselves that we must not only practice forgiveness, we are the recipients of forgiveness. Most of us have been forgiven by family, friends and perhaps by our communities. All of us are recipients of God's forgiveness.

"I will study and get ready, and perhaps my chance will come."

—Abraham Lincoln

Everyone has opportunities. However, we are not always prepared to take advantage of them. Opportunities for education, careers, homes and families go unclaimed when we are not prepared to take title of them. "If only I hadda" is a familiar refrain.

In addition to becoming educated, we must also be prepared for opportunities for emotional and spiritual development. No one looks forward to an opportunity to forgive someone else. Yet, circumstances which call for forgiveness may be opportunities for personal growth. The practice of forgiveness requires us to take command of our feelings and choices we make.

Study and get ready to practice forgiveness. Be prepared; your chance to practice forgiveness will come many times over.

8

"Forgiveness takes courage and determination. Dig deep and you will find the strength you need."

—Forgiveness Therapy

Forgiving people are often belittled as weak by those who do not appreciate the strength needed to forgive. When mistreated by the class bully, children are taught to hit back. Those children who choose not to retaliate are humiliated.

Forgiveness is an important social problem-solving skill. In some situations, it is the only alternative to violence. But forgiveness requires determination. One must be willing to go counter to natural impulses and social pressures.

Forgiving people do not give up easily. Many have learned to be as determined to forgive as perpetrators are to hurt. Perpetrators always dig deep enough to find strength to injure others. Forgiving people have learned to dig deeply and tap the reservoirs of courage and determination which fuel forgiveness, healing, and growth.

Filing a Flight Plan

Airplane pilots generally file a flight plan. Even when flight plans are not required, a flight plan can prove valuable. A flight plan includes a point of departure, proposed route, and destination. If the plane is lost, officials have a reasonable idea where to look.

A little planning may prevent us from losing sight of our needs to forgive. Some planning guidelines include:

1. Do not justify the perpetrator's misbehavior. We forgive what others do wrong; not what they do right.
2. Do not minimize the pain we feel. The pain is real.
3. Do not accept blame. (Of course we all need to forgive ourselves, but that is another flight plan.)
4. Know exactly what you are forgiving for that is your ultimate destination.

10 *The Cost of Picking Up the Pieces*

Repair costs are sometimes prohibitive. Automobiles involved in rather minor accidents may cost more to repair than they are worth. Yet, an antique automobile in poor condition may be worth complete restoration at considerable expense.

Of course, people are more valuable than durable goods. Yet, we are subject to serious damage.

When our lives are shattered, we may have difficulty thinking about repair. Indeed, some damage may be forgivable but not repairable.

An ancient prophet once wrote, "Where there is no vision the people perish." Without a vision, we may perish in our own destruction. Forgiveness provides us with the vision needed to pick up the pieces and mend the damage in our hearts.

Emotional bitterness not only hurts; it is self-defeating.

Bitterness may be a natural reaction to victimization, but natural reactions can be destructive. To a person lost at sea, drinking sea water may seem the natural thing to do. But in reality, drinking sea water only intensifies one's thirst. At first, bitterness may even seem comforting. Bitterness may supply us with endless fantasies of getting even. Yet, bitterness is costly. Consider the following:

1. Hatred toward parents can wreck a marriage.
2. Hostility can cause depression.
3. Self-pity drives friends away.
4. Anger can exacerbate panic attacks, migraine headaches, cardiovascular symptoms, and gastrointestinal disorders.

Maybe forgiveness is not so difficult after all.

Why forgive?

The simple answer to the question "why?" is "why not?" Of course this is an oversimplification, but it is an interesting thought.

Children in early childhood endlessly ask, "Why?" This is an important stage in their development. They are seeking new information. "Why?" is a good question and deserves a good answer.

Why should we forgive when we have been assailed? Because forgiveness is in our own best interest.

Carol Luebering wrote, "Let's get one thing straight; forgiving is not something we do for someone else. It is not even something you do because you should, according to the standards of religious belief or human decency. Forgiveness is something you do for yourself."

Why should we forgive? Why not!

What if that were me?

Modern media regularly provides us with short snippets of the misery of human victimization. Television vignettes show live close-up pictures of tears and raw agony.

Such media exposure may be an invasion of emotional intimacy. But, in the comfort of our living rooms, we regularly witness the pangs of those who have lost family members, or children in terrorist attacks.

Occasionally, out of the ashes of such cruelty, someone talks about forgiveness. No one suggests terrorists should be pardoned, but a few share their own quest for personal forgiveness.

Recovering alcoholics often repeat, "There but by the grace of God go I." With that in mind, consider those who suffer such terrible brutality. With compassion ask, "What if that were me!"

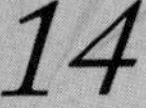

Motivation: The Motor of Forgiveness

St. Paul wrote, "When I was a child, I spoke as a child, I understood as a child, I thought as a child: but when I became a man, I put away childish things." Children are often motivated by fear. Unfortunately, fear is not restricted to children. Sometimes adults forgive because they fear the consequences of not forgiving. As we mature, our motivation should also mature. Forgiving out of fear is not as mature as forgiving from the heart. Essentially, there are two forms of motivation. *External motivation* is based on fear. We drive the speed limit because we fear getting a ticket. Internal motivation is based on our values. We drive the speed limit because we value the safety of ourselves and others.

Forgiveness motivated by the heart is genuine. We forgive simply because it is the right thing to do.

"Birds of a feather flock together."

Those familiar with teenagers know the most powerful influence on teenagers is other teenagers. The influence teenagers have on each other far exceeds the influence of their parents. Teens who associate with delinquents are at risk. Those who associate with leaders, exhibit leadership qualities.

Social influence is not limited to teenagers. Like birds of a feather, we tend to associate with people who are like us. Angry people tend to associate with angry people. Conversely, forgiving people tend to associate with loving people.

The influence we exert on those around us is determined by the person we choose to be.

Birds choose neither their feathers nor their flock. Human beings choose both.

16 *Fear of Loneliness*

Human beings are gregarious. Hermits are rather rare. Theologians tell us God created people for fellowship, which implies even God will not tolerate loneliness.

Basic social needs include personal affirmation and the need to be understood by others. When hurt and angry, we tend to gravitate toward other hurt and angry people hoping for affirmation and understanding. Since hurt and angry people fill these needs, we may hold onto them tenaciously.

Fearing loneliness may also restrain us from confronting those who abuse us. We may reason that to be close to an abusive person is better than loneliness.

In reality, forgiveness leads to overcoming loneliness. Forgiveness puts us in contact with spiritual fellowship with God and with forgiving people who truly understand our feelings.

Soar with Eagles or Flop with Turkeys

Eagles symbolize freedom and strength. Turkeys end up in sandwiches the day after Thanksgiving. In terms of lifestyle, eagles succeed at their jobs, have happy homes, enjoy good friends, and tend to be leaders. Turkeys are forever creating excuses for their self-defeating lives. Eagles are in control; turkeys are controlled.

Turkey behaviors are attempts to overcome felt inadequacy and compensate for loss of self-esteem. Turkeys perceive forgiveness as weakness. Eagles are not exempt from anger and frustration. Yet, they have confidence in themselves. They assume responsibility for their own feelings and behavior. For them, forgiveness is a sign of strength.

Fortunately, turkeydom teaches survival skills which are adaptable to eaglehood. Forgiveness is a catalyst in the metamorphosis from turkey to eagle.

18

"Courage is resistance to fear, mastery of fear—not absence of fear."

—Mark Twain

Only a fool has no fear. Fear is natural. Without fear we could not survive. However, uncontrolled levels of fear may restrict our lives. In extreme cases, fears escalate into phobias.

Forgiveness can be a fearful experience. We risk losing power generated by anger. We risk social ridicule by those who perceive forgiveness as weakness. We may fear the perpetrator will interpret our forgiveness as vulnerability.

The absence of fear would expose us to unnecessary physical and emotional dangers. Fear is mastered by courage tempered with mature judgment.

Forgiveness requires courage. The risks are real. Yet, strength is available to all of us. When fearful, recall the courage of King David who wrote, "Yea, though I walk through the valley of the shadow of death, I will fear no evil: For thou art with me..."

"I joked about every prominent man in my lifetime, but I never met one I didn't like."

—Will Rogers

Humor can be healing. In fact, the careful and appropriate use of humor may be very helpful for certain types of depression.

Yet, humor can be cruel. Unforgiving spiteful people may use humor to mock others. There is always a difference between laughing *with* a person and laughing *at* a person's expense. A forgiving spirit helps us make that distinction.

Forgiveness restores a balance in humor. Self-forgiveness permits us to comfortably laugh at ourselves. Forgiving others opens hearts and allows us to laugh with them.

Never joke in a manner you would not appreciate yourself. Remember, healthy humor should be used to bond with others, not to barb them.

20

"What an absurd thing it is to pass over all the valuable parts of a man, and fix our attention on his infirmities."

—Joseph Addison

Bearing animosity toward another person keeps us focused on the wrongdoing of that person. The sight or mention of that person floods our minds and hearts with his or her misdeeds.

Withholding forgiveness blocks our appreciation for any positive attributes an offender might possess. For example, a young husband and father lost a considerable amount gambling. He made a terrible mistake. Friends and family demonized him. They overlooked his love for his family and only focused on his error. Fortunately, he overcame his lapse in judgment, but forgiveness from those he loved took a long time.

Forgiveness helps us catch a vision of an offender's potential, much like God must see us when we make mistakes.

"Everyone is eagle-eyed to see another's faults."

—John Dryden

Most of us are experts at finding faults in other people. Children often learn no one pays attention to them unless they do something wrong. Some specialists on parenting suggest if parents would spend equal time telling children what they do right, punishment would seldom be necessary. Nevertheless, some children grow into adults getting attention by mistreating others.

To be a fault-finding nitpicker requires no special skills. Sometimes the only way fault-finders can feel good about themselves is criticizing others and feeling superior by comparison.

Truly great people spotlight the strengths of other people. Faults can be forgiven. What would the world be like if there were more strength-finders than fault-finders?

22

"How immense appear to us the sins we have not committed."

—Madame Necker

Most of us tend to justify our own misconduct.

Most people believe in the Ten Commandments. Yet, none of us is able to follow each and every Commandment. In an effort to justify our behavior, we tend to rearrange the commandments into a personal hierarchy of importance. Those we follow are important; those we break are less important; those our enemies violate are very important.

With modern computers it is easy to cut and paste. The Commandments can be rearranged at will. But remember, the original Commandments were carved in stone. Compassionately forgiving ourselves may be a lot easier than re-carving the Commandments.

"I can easier teach twenty what were good to be done, than to be one of the twenty to follow my own teachings."

—Shakespeare

An old adage instructs, "Don't do as I do, do as I say do." Perhaps the greatest fear among parents is the fear our offspring will repeat our mistakes. For example, children of unwed parents are statistically more at risk for having children out of wedlock. Parents know by experience the consequcnces of unwise behavior.

In loving desperation we hope our children will follow our teachings and ignore our examples. We hope they will forgive, even though we have difficulty forgiving others.

We hold a high standard for our children because we love them. Is it fair we hold them to a higher standard than we ourselves live? No. Is it reasonable to expect them to overcome where we have failed? No. Is it equitable to expect them to love when we have exhibited hate? No. But maybe they will forgive us.

24 *"Each man can interpret another's experience only by his own."*

—Henry David Thoreau

Eleven-year-old Timmy suddenly developed a bad habit of stealing. He quickly learned to lie, covering himself.

Timmy's problem became progressively worse until he was asked if anyone had ever stolen from him. Timmy quickly recalled his bicycle had been stolen. He complained that those who had stolen his bicycle had lied about it. Eventually, Timmy got his bicycle back but it was damaged beyond repair.

With a little guidance from a caring adult, Timmy recalled how he felt when he was victimized. He now understood the pain he was creating for others. The stealing stopped.

Reaching inside ourselves to understand others may help us be more forgiving. We are simply one human being forgiving another.

"Our anxiety turns to rage because, as a criminal psychologist once told me, rage is a more tolerable human emotion than fear."

—Patricia Pearson

Many of us were taught that all anger is inappropriate. Not so. Anger is the appropriate response when we see someone (including ourselves) being abused or mistreated, when rights are being violated or human beings are being taken advantage of.

It is anger that puts us in touch with our bedrock beliefs and motivates us to challenge and change unhealthy situations in our lives.

26

"A wise man will make more opportunity than he finds."

—Francis Bacon

A wise person not only creates opportunities for himself or herself, a wise person takes advantage of those opportunities. Opportunities seldom fall into our laps. Yet, even unsolicited opportunities have little or no value unless we are willing to make something of them.

The travail of forgiveness may be a well-disguised opportunity. Certainly such opportunities are not welcomed. Yet, the true temper of our character is often forged on the anvil of our souls. What may appear as devastation, may be an opportunity to heal and grow. Such unsolicited pain may be an opportunity to extend love far beyond our present limits.

Is forgiving someone who has hurt us an opportunity? Depends on what we choose to make of it.

"All growth depends on activity. There is no development physically or intellectually without effort, and effort means work."

—Calvin Coolidge, *Leaves of Gold*

Sigmund Freud was once asked, what in his opinion, were the most important principles of life. He replied, "love and work." To simply love is not enough. Love must be expressed to be meaningful. For example, parents love their children, but express that love by supporting and caring for them.

Forgiveness promotes healing and growth in proportion to the effort we are willing to invest. Casual forgiveness produces casual growth. Serious forgiveness is labor intensive. For instance, the level of forgiveness needed to save a marriage may be exhausting but most rewarding.

Forgiveness is a labor of love. It is symptomatic of a healthy love for ourselves and a commitment to maturing into the person God intends for us to be.

28

"I complained about having no shoes until I met a man who had no feet."

Victims are naturally concentrated on the intensity of their own pain. Indeed, victimization hurts and attention to our pain is normal and unavoidable. When in the throes of agony over being hurt, it is easy to forget others hurt too.

Sometimes experiencing deep pain and anger equips us to understand those who, like us, are in pain. The pain of victimization tends to be lonely. Sympathy helps little, if at all. Understanding provides healing through compassionate human support.

Time feeling sorry for ourselves is generally wasted. A more productive use of time might be to share the strength we have found in forgiveness with those who may be in deeper pain.

Some of the nicest people are hypocrites.

Hypocrites get a bad rap. Nobody wants to be a hypocrite or even associated with them. Yet, maybe being a hypocrite is not so bad after all. By definition a hypocrite is one who believes and teaches a high standard but does not himself or herself live up to that standard. For instance, most of us believe in the Ten Commandments or the Sermon on the Mount. Yet, we consistently fail to live up to such standards.

Some complain the church is full of hypocrites. But is there a better place for hypocrites? Barring hypocrites from church is tantamount to barring sick people from hospitals.

The next time you see a genuine hypocrite, forgive that person. For in all likelihood you are standing in front of a mirror.

When We Are Angry at God

For many, the thought of being angry at God is beyond comprehension. Yet, most people experience anger at God but may not be able to consciously admit it. Such underlying anger may erode the quality of our spiritual lives.

For example, when children die, parents may take their anger out on each other when they are actually angry at God.

God's forgiveness is a beacon to His love. Certainly our anger does not destroy God's love for us. Genuine faith allows us to acknowledge our anger toward God and clearly express our feelings to Him.

Earthly parents and children routinely resolve anger. How much more will our Heavenly Father who is the source of all love and forgiveness accept our anger and heal our wounds.

The more we invest in our own growth and development, the more we have to give to others.

A middle-aged man came to a life changing realization and exclaimed, "If I were someone else, I would want me for a friend; forgiving myself made me that way." Through self-forgiveness, he could accept himself even if others could not.

Most of us are uncomfortable with our inherent worth as human beings. For example, try a simple experiment: First, pick three people and give each person a compliment. Next, pick three different people and tell them something special about yourself. Most people find the first part of the experiment much easier than the latter.

Forgiving ourselves is an important investment in our personal growth. Self-forgiving people make wonderful friends for they are prepared to forgive our shortcomings as well.

June

"He is like a cow that gives a good bucket of milk, then turns around and kicks it over."

—Folk saying heard in West Alabama

Most of us would like to be judged on the basis of our intentions rather than our behavior. Unfortunately, this is rarely the case. But do our intentions count at all? Of course they do. Intentions are from the heart. Sometimes our behaviors are not consistent with our intentions.

Our intentions are deeply personal and not readily appreciated by others. We might intend to give a good bucket of milk; we do not intend to kick it over. The world will judge us for kicking the bucket over, but we know in our hearts our intentions were honorable.

Recognizing our honorable intentions makes forgiving ourselves much easier. At peace with ourselves, we allow those who judge us more severely to cry over the spilled milk.

2 *Forgiveness*

—John Greenleaf Whittier

"One summer Sabbath day I strolled
    among
The green mounds of the village burial-
    place;
Where pondering how all human love
    and hate
Find one sad level; and how, soon or
    late,
Wronged and Wrongdoer, each with
    meekened face,
and cold hands folded over a still heart,
Pass the green threshold of our com-
    mon grave,
Whither all footsteps tend, whence
    none depart,
Awed for myself, and pitying my race,
Our common sorrow, like a mighty
    wave,
Swept all my pride away, and trembling
    I Forgave!"

Angels Unaware

3 JUNE

Sometimes we may encounter angels only to comprehend their message long after they have gone. For instance, a forty-year-old man was diagnosed with terminal cancer. His doctors advised him he had less than a year to live. Rather than becoming consumed with anger, he began spiritually and emotionally preparing his family and making provisions for them.

Yet, tragedy continued to haunt this courageous man. During the year he had left, his wife suddenly died. A few weeks later his son was killed in an accident.

The last months of his life were a monument to the human spirit of forgiveness. He never lost sight of love and caring. He continually inspired all who had the privilege of knowing him. Then he was gone. Was he an angel? Angels are messengers. What a powerful message he left behind!

Doing Our Best

An eighteen-year-old young lady was faced with high school tests which could effect her future. She became extremely anxious and suffered sleepless nights, loss of appetite, and dread someone would think she was not intelligent.

Finally, a teacher who knew the young lady, expressed assurance. The teacher explained, "I am confident you will do your very best. Doing our best is all that can be expected. There is dignity in doing our best and that dignity is beyond measurement of any test."

The young lady's anxiety immediately lifted. She was confident she would do her best. Her dignity and worth as a person would be intact regardless of her test scores.

In life we are tested when others violate our dignity. Forgiveness may be the only thing we can do; it might also be the very best we can do.

"Judge not thy friend until thou standest in his place."

—Rabbi Hillel

Those who have made few mistakes, or at least those who only acknowledge having made few mistakes, are generally more harsh in their judgment of others. For instance, one might harshly denounce a prostitute without understanding she may have been driven in desperation for food and shelter. Those who have experienced cold and hunger may not condemn so quickly.

Circumstances do not necessarily justify behavior. Yet, understanding one's circumstances may temper our judgment with compassion.

Drawing from the reservoir of our own failures may give us an appreciation for compassion. A spirit of forgiveness never seeks to condemn. A spirit of forgiveness is always willing to share with others the compassion we have found, or at least wanted to find, in our own failures.

6 *"The members of the human race who move me most to scornful diction, are sensitive and injured souls luxuriating in affliction."*

—Rebecca McCann, Cheerful Cherub

Victims' rights is a healthy movement. For too long criminals have violated the basic rights of others, leaving their victims without recourse. What happens to those who are permanently injured or brain damaged after robberies and muggings? Who pays for the therapy of victims of rape, especially when they would rather die than resolve their feelings of degradation?

Forgiveness is not something we do for another; rather, we do it for ourselves, for peace of mind and for growth. Perpetrators may or may not know of the forgiveness; it is the exclusive domain of victims.

Victims are entitled to rage, frustration, and bitterness. Without the right to seethe in anger, we would have no need to forgive. But as victims we also have the right and responsibility to move on to forgiveness.

The Human Struggle

Hate poisons; forgiveness heals. It's that simple—or is it? Why not stop where we are, use this simple truth, and begin growing into loving, mature, warm human beings? What a beautiful idea, but in real life we must deal with the fact that we are, indeed, human beings.

Human hatred knows no bounds. In his book, *The Nazi Doctors*, Robert J. Lifton struggled with "...the disturbing psychological truth that ... ordinary people can commit demonic acts."

While human hatred knows no bounds, God's love is also limitless. From His love we learn forgiveness. There is no known cure for being human. But we can act better. Human beings have the capacity for love, healing, and growth.

Therapeutic Forgiveness—An Open Secret

Therapeutic forgiveness is such a powerful dynamic one might wonder why it is so commonly ignored. Those in professional practice have little understanding or appreciation of forgiveness as a healing tool in therapy.

Relegating forgiveness to the domain of religion, psychotherapists rarely incorporate it into clinical practice and, unfortunately, only a few spiritual leaders appreciate its psychotherapeutic value. Frequently, spiritual leaders focus on our need to be forgiven rather than our need to practice the skill of forgiveness. Of course, we all need to be forgiven but we also need to learn how to forgive. The personal discovery and exercise of therapeutic forgiveness, then, may be a lonely, largely unexplored one.

But take heart; therapeutic forgiveness does work!

The Impact of Forgiveness on Personality

Psychotherapists often concentrate on personality. Briefly summarized, personality is what we present to the world; it is how we see ourselves and how others see us from first impressions to the lasting impact we make on those we love. Personality is the sum of who we are.

Young people often cite "personality" as the most important opposite-sex attraction. Unfortunately, many attractive personalities are severely dysfunctional.

All we think, feel, believe, and do is filtered through our personalities. Personality, when allowed to ferment in anger and hostility, becomes malignant and bitter. Personality, when infused with forgiveness, becomes loving.

10 *Forgiveness? Not Me!*

"Maybe if I hate enough I'll be happy." While this attitude does not make sense, nonetheless, many fear giving it up will separate them forever from their hope for happiness. Before becoming too critical, we should understand that resisting forgiveness is a normal protective mechanism.

Most mechanisms block healing and growth. Yet, we acquire mechanisms for good reasons. The main reason is survival, not necessarily physical but certainly emotional. Early in life we learn to use frustration and anger to command attention and make certain we are fed and sustained.

Forgiveness may seem contrary to our basic mechanisms.

When overwhelmed with resistance, remember resistance is normal and forgivable.

Forgiveness Perceived as a Loss of Power

Most of us feel we have little or no control over our lives and that our lives are over-regulated. Realistically, few of us control our communities, jobs, or taxes. We may, perhaps, have marginal control over our families, but divorce, reported abuse, and the ever-increasing power of growing children limit even this control.

Understandably, we seek a few areas of life we can control. These areas affirm our autonomy and control makes us feel like real people when, in reality, we have only diminished ourselves.

We tend to equate hate with strength and love with weakness. We become vulnerable with too much love while hate, on the other hand, offers a sense of self-protection. It serves to keep others at bay. We perceive forgiveness as "wimpish," but those who can forgive find untold strength of character.

“But I don’t want to love that awful person.”

Harboring hatred gives the illusion of controlling those who have abused us and gives hope for vengeance. With enough resentment, the offender will surely change. This is a delusion, of course, but it gives us a sense of power over those who crush us. Hate is so easy.

The idea of mystical power emerging from thoughts and feelings has a long tradition. The ancient Hebrews believed that certain verbal pronouncements released powers to accomplish the spoken word.

We cannot control the behavior of other people, but we can withhold forgiveness, believing that our hostility will intimidate them. Unwittingly, our attempt to control others by hating robs us of self-control. Our own bitterness becomes our adversary.

Holier Than Thou

Some people shy away from forgiveness associating it with pious religious groups who perceived themselves as too righteous to associate with the rest of us sinners. Of course, there are some genuinely saintly people, but they usually understand the struggles experienced by the rest of us.

Non-forgiveness is an illusion that fosters the need to put down offenders. After all, such reasoning goes, offenders are evil and should be put in their place.

Genuine forgiveness demands that we relinquish the delusion of moral superiority, in spite of our hope to hold onto our "right" to complain, belittle, and attack. Forgiveness strips us of the satisfaction we gain by demeaning others and lording it over them. It is natural to want the power to knock others down; it is not natural to pick up the gauntlet of loving compassion.

Abuse Viewed as Love

Children often confuse love and abuse when those who are supposed to love them abuse them. Some of these children grow into adults who abuse others or subject themselves to further abuse in adult life. Many in state prisons were victimized as children. Others find themselves involved in self-destructive domestic relationships.

As children, most of us experienced guilt and eventually confessed so we could be punished and feel better. It worked in childhood, but it can be devastating in adult life. The misperception is that if we forgive we must hold onto self-punishing behaviors we have always hoped would make us feel better.

Therapeutic forgiveness separates abuse and love. No one needs to be subjected to hurt as the price for love. Abuse produces victims; love generates growth.

Most of us allow our feelings to override our better judgment.

Reckless, irresponsible behaviors are often exhibited by intelligent people who have allowed themselves to become so steeped in anger their emotions have fermented into self-defeating behaviors which are no longer controlled by their own rational processes. For example, most teenagers who become addicted to drugs are experts on the dangers of substance abuse. Other teenagers start failing in school hoping to capture needed love and attention.

While clear thinking and forgiveness are not the same, rational thinking can help us through the confusing maze of our angry emotions. Clear thinking helps us understand the power of forgiveness.

16 *Dread of Reconciliation*

Does forgiveness mean we must love someone we now hate? Few of us want to give up the perverse joy of nursing hatred. Being repulsed by someone who has hurt us is normal. In some cases, being close to that person could be traumatic.

Fortunately, however, true forgiveness does not imply that we become doormats for thoughtless or mean people. On the other hand, today's oppressive, inconsiderate nincompoop could be tomorrow's valued friend. Forgiveness opens that possibility.

One of the most difficult steps toward emotional maturity is learning to love the unlovable. Christian belief stresses God's love for everyone. This is an esoteric ideal, but some of us manage to get better by letting go of hate. At least it promises more fertile soil for love to grow.

Roadblock: Fear of Our Own Internal Rage

Fear of the intensity of our own anger may cause us to resist forgiveness. Though we may act civilized, deep inside there can be raging emotional volcanoes. This is dangerous because "good" people do not explode or even allow themselves to get teed off.

For example, a sixteen-year-old boy accumulated a long history of fighting, poor school performance, and threatening adults. The young man had been removed from his home. Attempts to place him with relatives failed resulting in even more rejection. Even shelters and group homes rejected him.

Finally, with guidance he was able to express his rage toward his mother. He found he could still love someone who had cruelly abused and rejected him.

18 *Fear of Sharing Too Much*

Most of us fear uncovering our internal rages. This fear, however, is mild when it is compared with sharing those feelings with someone else. If we cannot trust ourselves with these outcasts of the soul, who can we trust?

Maybe someone will understand and hold our feelings in trust. Healing often begins when we finally open ourselves to another person. Such sharing can be alarming since we become vulnerable and risk more hurt in honest self-disclosure. Choosing the right confidant is crucial and trust is essential.

Forgiveness takes place inside ourselves. There are no prerequisites from any other person—especially the perpetrator. No one need ever know whom you have forgiven—or why. However, others may witness beautiful changes in your life and you will find peace.

The cost of forgiving becomes more poignant with the realization we must accept the consequences of another's unjust behavior. We may suffer pain because someone has wreaked havoc in our lives—in our souls. Often we cannot repair the damage even if the perpetrator chooses to do so. Commonly, the perpetrator does not care how we feel, no matter how much we suffer.

To forgive an offense requires that we pay the price of accepting internal distress for another's behavior. We must assume undeserved hurt and give up hope for retaliation. Yes, it is unfair, but unfairness is a part of life. After all, if it were fair we would have no need to forgive.

20

"Instead of weeping when a tragedy occurs in a songbird's life, it sings away its grief. I believe we could well follow the pattern of our feathered friends."

—Robert S. Walker

Someone once said that anger is the first emotion we experience in our lives and the last one we learn how to manage effectively. So, in a sense, it comes down to Acceptance. If we are human, we are going to be angry. The only way to eliminate anger is to become so personally secure that nothing in the world threatens us. In lieu of that supernatural reality, for most of us that means working ever harder at peacefully resolving our anger, while accepting anger itself as a fact of life.

"I'll never rest until justice is done."

Justice is illusive and fickle. To base mental, emotional, and spiritual health on fairness is folly. Many of us grew up under the influence of Hopalong Cassidy, Superman, and Howdy Doody. We expect the bad guys to lose and the good to win.

Some believe good and evil must balance. The old idiom, "What goes around comes around," expresses the idea that someone must pay for every evil act. When victimized, we expect justice. We do not want to forgive and relinquish our hope of getting even. Ironically, we often lose interest in justice when we are the perpetrator.

Some wrongs cannot be made right. For instance, a damaged reputation may be irreparable. Our only option may be to forgive and repair our hearts.

22 *When Self-esteem Has Been Crushed*

When we are victimized, we feel powerless, violated, and angry. If we had more power, more resources, more intelligence, we could set the record straight. If we are attacked, we feel worthless. Victimization is an assault on our personal dignity. Yet, it does not erode our person or affect personal worth. But until this is understood, the idea of giving up revenge is unthinkable.

Forgiveness does not mean we continue to be victimized or fail to take legal recourse to assure others will not be victimized. We can, indeed, forgive and resolve bitterness and still take whatever steps necessary to execute justice. However, motivation need not be rooted in anger or hope of vengeance. That is spiritual and emotional poison.

Recognizing the Need to Forgive

One reason we overlook forgiveness as a cure for personal bitterness is our inability to recognize a need for it. Hostility may be disguised so well it is not seen as an emotional or spiritual disorder. Bitterness can creep slowly into our lives and become a part of our personalities. Unwittingly, we host parasites of emotional and spiritual disease that exist as long as they are allowed to live in us.

Recognizing the need to forgive does not come naturally. Anger and hate upset the balance of emotional homeostasis and lead to terminal bitterness. Forgiveness as a therapeutic intervention is not always a pleasant process.

There is no substitute for absolute self-honesty. Those who learn to forgive are brave and strong people who courageously call their own bitterness by its right name and venture to conquer it.

24 *All parents make mistakes.*

Parents have unimaginable influence on their children. We can do a lot of damage but we can also prevent much misery. The irony is that about the time we become grandparents we have finally learned to parent.

Some parents blame children for family dysfunction. These parents find it unthinkable to admit their need for improvement. They reshape reality and make the child responsible for the family's misery.

For many youngsters who grow up in these circumstances, forgiveness is irrelevant. They see nothing to forgive and cannot imagine life any other way. They grow up, choose dysfunctional mates, and clone their parents, misery and all. Yet, those who do find the power of forgiveness build homes of their own where love and mutual respect become a part of family heritage.

Incorporating Forgiveness into Early Childhood Development

Infants look to their parents and families for safety and security. The family environment is a school from which infants develop lifelong values and make early attempts to understand their place in the schema of the universe.

Most children love to hear about themselves and learn about their infancy. They are often spellbound when parents talk about early developmental accomplishments. They love to hear about their learning to crawl, walk, talk, and when their first tooth appeared.

Developmental psychologists tell us considerable programming takes place early in our existence. Important developmental milestones such as bonding, trust, and self-awareness precede memory. Each of these milestones should be carefully nurtured, for they provide the foundation for love and forgiveness.

26 *Early Development Revisited*

During the early developmental stages of life, we as children learn specific coping and problem-solving skills which shape our personalities and affect the direction of our lives.

Sigmund Freud theorized that neurotic or hysterical behavior has its roots in the development of personality which takes place long before we are aware of ourselves. Consequently, several generations blame their problems on inept parents, mysterious libidinal forces, or faulty potty training.

However, this does not imply that we cannot change who we are, what we are, what we are doing, and where we are going. We will always be responsible for ourselves. Of course our parents made mistakes. We begin taking command of our lives by forgiving them and praying our children will forgive us.

Teaching Children Forgiveness

The lack of parental discipline is common among disturbed children. When parents are "too busy," older siblings may attempt to take on parental responsibility for younger brothers and sisters, but they lack the needed authority or wisdom to be consistent.

The earlier forgiveness is learned, the less traumatic the lessons. Children have more difficulty recognizing the need to forgive, but they find forgiveness easier once they realize the need. Adults are better at recognizing the need, but they have more difficulty putting forgiveness into practice.

Teaching children the practice of forgiveness is an excellent investment in their future. Such an investment may be even more important than a college fund. After all, some educated people are grown up maladapted children with a diploma.

Teenagers are anxious to become men and women. Fifteen-year-olds usually think they are twenty while their parents see them as being no more than twelve. It is a confusing but wonderful period of life. Adolescence is a time when young men and women firm their concepts of masculinity and femininity. This is an excellent time to teach emotional maturity.

Remarkably, most teenagers with guidance can conduct themselves in an extraordinarily mature manner. They also respond to adult recognition of their mature qualities. Sometimes, teenagers behave more maturely than adults.

To grow into real men and women also includes emotional and spiritual growth. People who learn to forgive are men and women who stand as stalwart examples for us all.

Teaching Adults Forgiveness

As grown-ups, we use adult freedom to express anger, fury, venom, and malice. With more power, we become increasingly able to inflict our bitterness on ourselves and others. The need to learn and practice forgiveness becomes more urgent.

Adults who have not learned self-discipline can no longer look to parents to fill the deficit. One must learn it for oneself. Some experts refer to this as "re-parenting" ourselves. For instance, if we do not learn forgiveness in childhood, we must teach it to ourselves. Self-discipline strengthens us to achieve a more rewarding level of forgiveness and personal maturation.

Having to teach ourselves to be forgiving may be difficult, but it certainly prepares us to teach our children while their hearts are still open.

30 *Teaching Forgiveness in Our Homes*

Children need to be taught healthy expressions of anger. It is not an exclusive right of adulthood nor will it be eradicated in children by denying them expression. Some teaching guidelines include:

1. Set an example. Emotional hysteria is usually learned behavior.
2. Realize and accept the fact children get angry. It is normal.
3. Establish a cool-down period. You and the children need it.
4. Encourage healthy expression. It is okay to be angry; it is not okay to be disrespectful or destructive.
5. Be consistent. You may disagree with their feelings but be ready to understand. Do not forget to pray for wisdom and forgive yourself when you make mistakes.

JULY

A Sharper Picture: Focus on Forgiveness

Forgiveness is only a concept until we personalize it by forgiving specific violations which have been committed against us. Once the perpetrator and the violation are clear, we have sharpened the picture to the exclusion of other areas of anger or bitterness which may lay buried in our hearts. We need not assume blame for the misbehavior of others. Clearly recognizing how someone else has hurt us is an honest way of dealing with our true feelings.

Inside, each of us may be angry at different people for different reasons. The challenge is to sharpen the picture until we become aware of whom and what we need to forgive. We may help one another, but we must each sharpen the image of our own personal feelings and accept clear responsibility for our personal need to forgive.

Passive-aggression is no substitute for genuine forgiveness.

Passive-aggression is a backwards way of expressing anger. Procrastination, doing a job but doing it poorly, sulking and silence are ways of expressing anger in non-aggressive yet irritating ways. Passive-aggressive behaviors range from stubbornness in children to full-blown personality disorders in adults.

Passive-aggressive people see no need to forgive others. The passive-aggressive person hides anger under indifference and may appear pious, innocent, and victimized. In reality, passive-aggression is a means of expressing hostility. It is belligerent, retaliatory behavior; an indicator that forgiveness is in short supply.

Passive-aggressive people are indeed maddening. Yet, keep in mind they too are in need of our forgiveness.

Assess the mess.

When we assess the mess, it becomes clear that our emotions—perhaps our lives—have been laid waste by the malicious behavior of someone else. But the real mess is what is happening in us, not what someone else has done to us. Without serious intervention, the mess gets worse; bitterness is born.

Failure to forgive can cause more damage than the original offense. The fact that we have been damaged is validation for the need to forgive.

Fortunately, assessing emotional wreckage can bring about a renewed human spirit. There is always hope for rebuilding. Forgiven bitterness can be bulldozed and buried. A new and better life is built atop the debris. Life is what you make.

4 *Appraising damage within ourselves is personal; repairing that damage is even more personal.*

Calamity is a tragic part of life. Wars, accidents, crimes, fires, floods, tornadoes, and hurricanes take heavy tolls. In shock, survivors wonder if life can continue, especially when loved ones are lost. Yet, a renewed strength emerges with a determination to rebuild along with compassion for other victims.

What is true for disaster victims is equally true when we are faced with forgiving someone who has left our lives in ruins.

Unresolved anger can ruin a marriage or sever parent/child relationships. Glossed over hostility can cause depression. Unexpressed anger may cause a host of cardiovascular and gastrointestinal disorders. Forgiveness may seem difficult, until we recapture the hope of rebuilding and getting better.

The Cost of Repairing the Damage of Someone Else's Behavior

When someone has hurt us, the cost of repair means we must pay to rebuild what someone else has destroyed. Forgiveness will cost our right to hate. We will have to relinquish priceless ammunition in our arsenal for retaliation. But what is the cost of an "eye for an eye"? If we have lost one eye, is it worth risking the other?

We may convince ourselves the cost of repair is not worth the effort. One cannot argue this point if the focus is on changing the offender. Attempting to change someone else is usually not cost effective.

Considering the cost can be dismaying because it is usually heavy. In the final analysis, however, the cost is nothing less than a long-term investment in ourselves. But forgiveness, growth, and healing pay handsome dividends.

6 *To Be or Not to Be; To Repair or Not to Repair*

Rebuilding in a flood-prone area may be chancy. Insurance companies calculate such risks with computers. But options are more limited when it comes to reconstructing lives.

Repair requires a blueprint; a vision of reconstruction. It may be hard to imagine life sans bitterness. Some may never have known any other way. It is helpful to find another person who exemplifies a forgiving spirit. No one is perfect, but the world is filled with wonderful people whose lives confirm that the price is worthwhile. They give us hope. Perhaps we may recapture a vision of better times from the past. Marriage counselors often ask couples to recall their happiness when they were dating. The challenge is to regain that happiness. It was possible once; it could be possible again.

"The masterful mind is always positive."

—O.S. Marden, *Conquest of Worry*

For many years the renowned pastor Dr. Norman Vincent Peale wrote about and taught the power of positive thinking. Dr. Peale was aware of the detrimental effects of negative thinking. To be sure, the quality of our thinking affects the quality of our feelings which affects the quality of our lives.

Anger, resentment, hate, and spite are common examples of negative thinking and feelings. These thoughts and feelings require no special skills. Like weeds, they seem to grow and choke out such positive characteristics as love, caring, and forgiveness.

Cultivating positive characteristics requires positive thinking. Positive thinking is no more than self-discipline. Self-discipline takes patience and practice.

8

"An able man shows his spirit by gentle words and absolute actions."

—Phillip Dormer Chesterfield

Anger tends to be expressed in loud, hostile tones. One family therapist frequently asks children, "Who is the champion screamer at your house?" The answers tend to embarrass parents but prove productive. The therapist then asks, "What can be done in your home to reduce the yelling?" Sometimes the children provide such profound answers, the therapist is no longer needed.

When families practice a forgiving spirit, the impulse to use harsh tones is sharply reduced. Forgiving home environments are more tranquil. No family is free of conflicts. But in homes where love, caring, respect, and forgiveness are exercised, notable differences can be observed. These differences include: fewer arguments; when arguments occur they are resolved quickly; intense arguments are very rare.

"The man who never makes mistakes never makes anything. Many chips, broken instruments, cuts and bruises, belong to the history of a beautiful statue. Persist in spite of everything."

—Maltbie D. Babcock

In Egypt there are many ancient pyramids. One of the earliest is called the Broken Pyramid. Apparently the structure broke during construction. The pyramid was completed but at an altered angle of ascent. Learning from mistakes, more elaborate pyramids were built.

Sometimes, our ability to forgive seems to break down. We may feel our broken ability to forgive, like the Broken Pyramid, stands as a monument to failure.

The Broken Pyramid was not a total failure. In spite of being broken, it has stood for thousands of years. Fortunately, broken forgiveness can be repaired more easily than a broken pyramid. We may need more time to heal. We may need to open our hearts. When forgiveness seems to break, remember the Egyptians continued learning and continued building.

10

"A man that seeks truth and loves it must be reckoned precious to any human society."

—Frederick the Great

The truth is sometimes hard to love. The truth about ourselves can prove painfully difficult. For instance, facing our own failures or the internal hurt of having been betrayed can be agonizing.

In a book titled, *A Guide to Recovery*, the authors cite a proverb which expresses the dilemma of facing the truth of our pain, "The truth will make you free, but first it will make you miserable."

Each of us must accept the pain of having been hurt. Even though the emotional support of others may be helpful, we cannot shift the responsibility for coping with our pain onto others.

Assuming clear ownership of our pain clarifies our need to forgive. Regardless of who caused the pain, the hurt abides within us. The truth tells us that only we ourselves can heal the pain by forgiving those who hurt us.

"The more someone knows, the more someone forgives."

—Anonymous

Most of us have found ourselves saying, "If I had only known then what I know now." With present knowledge, we might have been more forgiving. The better we know a person, the more we know their faults. The more we understand another's behavior, the more we have a basis for compassion.

But knowledge is no guarantee of forgiveness. Knowing more about the circumstances and behavior of others may intensify our anger. For instance, we may learn what we thought was unintentional was actually intentional and malicious.

Yet, knowledge may expedite wisdom. For example, we might find ourselves saying, "If I had only known then the power of forgiveness, I would have forgiven long ago."

12

"A well-ordered life is like climbing a tower; the view halfway up is better than the view from the base, and steadily becomes finer as the horizon expands."

—William Lyon Phelps

A group was climbing a particularly difficult mountain peak. Fatigue set in and the climbers tended to become discouraged. All they could see was where they had been and the face of the mountain in front of them. Finally, the leader reached the top. From his vantage point he described the beauty of this mountain top experience. Inspired by his description, the others soon joined him.

Sometimes, our anger, hurt, and rage loom so large in front of us we cannot see over or around our feelings. We may give up in bitterness and frustration before we reach the summit.

When we can see nothing but our own mountain of anger, look above. There are those who have climbed ahead. Keep in mind you too will have climbed the mountain and you too will encourage others to share the vistas of forgiveness.

Failing to forgive is forgivable.

When we hurt someone else, we hope they will forgive us. But this is not always the case. Sometimes those we offend will harbor resentment or even seek revenge. In turn, we may be hurt by their refusal to forgive. Yet, we need not allow resentment to build in our own hearts. Their refusal to forgive is forgivable. Sometimes our hearts are hard and angry. We may refuse to forgive and wallow in our own anger. We may need to forgive our own callousness before we can forgive others.

At other times, we may forgive, but our forgiveness is less than perfect. We may be surprised to find old angers resurfacing. Remember we are imperfect human beings. As such, our forgiveness cannot always be perfect. Imperfect forgiveness, like imperfect people, is forgivable.

14 *Is it ever too late to forgive?*

An embittered middle-aged lady suddenly lost her husband. A few months later she was partially paralyzed by a stroke. Longstanding bitterness had driven away friends. She was now alone, embittered, and disabled.

Desperate, she began reaching out. Fortunately, she found strangers who befriended her. Slowly at first, she responded to their kindness. Eventually, she was able to forgive a lifetime of internal resentment and lived her last few years in peace.

Not everyone is so fortunate. As people live longer, more suffer various forms of senility. They may lose cognitive functions needed to understand and practice forgiveness.

When people lose the ability to forgive, we can always assure them of our forgiveness. Forgiveness assures we use our time well.

"One Nation Under God"

The War Between the States represents the darkest period in American history. States, friends, and families were divided against each other. Finally, the war came to a close. Rather than celebrate victory, Abraham Lincoln undertook to effect healing. His plan was not popular by those who sought revenge. Reconciliation would require forgiveness on both sides.

Due to Lincoln's untimely assassination, his plans were never fully implemented. Hatred and bitterness continued. Elements of those feelings remain till the present time.

Of course, forgiveness and reconciliation eventually mended our broken nation. Yet, we cannot help but wonder if healing would have been more immediate and more complete if forgiveness had been fully implemented in the early days of reconciliation.

16

"If your mind is saturated with fear, worry, discouragement, hatred, envy, jealousy, it has no room for the nobler emotions."

—O.S. Marden, *Conquest of Worry*

Sometimes our minds seem like overloaded computers. Yet, when the hard drive on our computers is filled to capacity we simply add more memory or replace our old computers with new and more powerful ones. However, replacing or upgrading our computers may not always be feasible. A possible alternative may be to delete unnecessary programs to make room for new ones.

When our minds become overloaded with anger and hostility we do not have the option of replacing our brains. Fortunately, we may be able to delete unwanted programs such as hate, hurt, and anger. These programs can be replaced with love, compassion and caring. How do we remove these unwanted programs from our minds? Forgiveness is your delete key.

"We believe Thou has the answers to all our problems, and yet we do not consult Thee."

—Peter Marshall

A fifty-two-year-old woman suddenly died. The cause of her death remained a mystery until a prescription for medication which would have saved her life was found in her purse.

In our hearts most of us know there are spiritual answers to our problems. Yet, such answers are frequently ignored. We may be drawn to the illusion of more immediate answers which include anger, resentment, and revenge.

Forgiveness is an attribute of God which He freely shares with each of us. Yet, when our hearts are filled with rage, we overlook the most important of all answers to the problems which disturb our souls.

Theologians tell us God breathed the breath of life into us. We need not search for answers to our problems. For His love, strength, and forgiveness are as close as the air we breathe.

18

*"Anger at another's fault I cannot honestly condone—
It's nearly always just a way we turn attention from our own."*

—Rebecca McCann, *Cheerful Cherub*

Reaction formation is a psychological term for a mechanism used by most of us from time to time. Simply explained, a reaction formation is an attempt to control our unacceptable urges and impulses by keeping the spotlight focused on others who act out our impulses. Our own impulses remain behind a smoke screen of sanctity.

For instance, one who becomes excessively concerned about the moral conduct of others may be struggling to control his or her own impulses.

Genuine forgiveness encourages an honest appraisal of our own behavior as well as the behavior of others. Spiritual, emotional, and psychological honesty replace pious smoke screens. Genuine forgiveness helps us become genuine people.

"Eat at your own table as you would eat at the table of the king."

—Confucius

Those who love us most deserve our best, but most often see our worst. We feel secure in our homes and less apt to be rejected. Yet, our homes often become combat zones filled with anger and warring factions.

The fact our deportment would be more appropriate in the presence of a king is evidence we are aware of proper codes of conduct.

Confucius understood the need to integrate ourselves. For a well-integrated person is comfortable at all socio-economic levels and in a wide range of social settings. The practice of forgiveness is an integrating experience. Anger, hurt, and outrageous behaviors are the domains of kings and paupers alike. Forgiveness invites the human race to a common table. This is one banquet you do not want to miss.

20

"The love principle is stronger than the force principle."

—A.A. Hodge

A young man was caught breaking into cars. Smashing windows he easily broke into one car after another. In a short time the young man caused a considerable amount of damage. Eventually he was caught by his own conscience and sought voluntarily to make restitution. Loving but firm parents provided support. No one forced him to make amends. His love for his parents and for himself prevailed.

When angry and upset we feel the urge to force apologies or restitution. On the other hand, forgiveness dissipates anger and calms our disquieted impulses.

No one can force forgiveness. We cannot force others to forgive us nor can anyone force us to forgive those who violate us. Genuine forgiveness is loving and always voluntary.

"Conduct is three-fourths of life."

—Matthew Arnold

A sixth-grader with a learning disability became increasingly frustrated with school. Observing that others seemed to learn faster and easier, he attempted to disrupt the class so the other students would not get too far ahead of him. Parents and teachers became more and more stymied. The principal threatened to expel the child. In desperation, his parents took the boy to a children's therapist.

The therapist explained the need to maintain proper conduct. He pointed out that children never get into serious trouble over grades; they get into trouble over conduct.

Improper conduct strains human relationships. The consequences of poor conduct can be severe. Unfortunately, none of us is perfect; which means forgiveness needs to play a very active part in our lives.

22

"A profound conviction raises a man above the feeling of ridicule."

—John Stuart Mills

Forgiving people are sometimes subject to ridicule. Forgiveness can be perceived as weak or passive by those who do not understand the strength and courage needed to practice forgiveness.

For example, Mahatma Gandhi was frequently ridiculed for his compassionate non-violent philosophy and life-style. Yet, Ghandi's inner strength has had an immeasurable impact on the world.

Some people seem naturally forgiving. They seem to have an inner depth of character. These are people who have made forgiveness a profound conviction. For them, forgiveness has been incorporated into the very core of their being.

Ironically, forgiving people are victimized again when they are ridiculed for practicing forgiveness. Somehow, forgiving people do not seem unusually affected by this. After all, ridicule is forgivable.

A centipede was happy quite until a frog in fun
Said, "Pray, which leg comes after which?"
This raised her mind to such a pitch,
She lay distracted in a ditch,
Considering how to run.

—Anonymous

Forgiveness can be very simplistic yet most complex. Hurt and angry people often cry out, "Tell me how to forgive!"

Forgiveness is an art and not always accomplished by a step by step technique. Like falling in love there are no established procedures. Any such rules would change from one circumstance to another. Forgiveness is much like painting a picture or writing a song. Forgiveness begins by allowing ourselves to feel pain. An artist mixes paints on a palette; a musician has endless scribbled notes. Yet, somehow feelings from the heart take shape on canvas or fill the air with music. Forgiveness begins with pain and confusion. Yet, when we open our hearts, forgiveness brings both color and harmony into our lives.

24

"We do not what we ought, what we ought not, we do;
and lean upon the thought, that change will bring us through."

—Matthew Arnold

Most of us have been at war with ourselves. We want to feel better; we want to do better. Yet, somehow we seem to sabotage our own best efforts.

Such conflicts remind us of that inner quality in each of us to be better people. The presence of conflict indicates we are not content to remain mired in our failures.

Sometimes chance will free us from the mire. Perhaps someone we have hurt will forgive us and lift us out of the doldrums of guilt. But chance is risky. We cannot always count on being forgiven. Fortunately we can take active command of our mistakes. We can forgive ourselves. We can make amends when possible. We can offer love and caring.

Perhaps our efforts will encourage forgiveness. While there are no guarantees at least there is a pretty good chance.

"Truth makes life a noble thing, and courage makes it strong, but grace and tact must set them off as music does a song."

—Rebecca McCann, *Cheerful Cherub*

Truly forgiving people seldom make a point of their forgiveness. They understand that to emphasize their forgiveness also emphasizes the misbehavior of the offender. Forgiveness is never accomplished at the expense of the transgressor.

Forgiveness takes place within our own hearts and does not require shame or remorse by those who have hurt us. While we may need to clarify how we have been hurt, offenders are due tactful respect. Hostile confrontation is not necessary. Indeed, true forgiveness hopes to preserve the dignity of the wrongdoer.

Forgiveness is noble but not boastful. Forgiveness is strong but not overbearing. Forgiveness often takes place with such quiet grace, only the forgiving person hears the music of restored peace.

26

"Nothing will stunt one's growth, and starve and strangle his vitality, like living in the constant atmosphere of worry.

—O.S. Marden, *Conquest of Worry*

Negative feelings are taxing. Such emotions as hostility, anxiety, worry, and depression seem to have a way of becoming pervasive. They often affect sleep, appetite, attitude, and social relationships. Over a period of time these feelings may take up permanent residence in the structure of our personalities. Negative feelings are not only taxing, they are toxic. Like parasites these feelings feed off the vitality of our souls.

Unresolved anger intensifies worry. Worry solves nothing. There is no healing value in worry. We may even worry about being so worried. Forgiveness offers freedom from negative feelings. Worry, anger, hate, and depression are lifted. We are restored to new vitality. We find new energy, new challenges, new directions.

"I believe in living up to the best that is in me. For to lower the standard is to give up the fight."

—Calvin Coolidge

To live in anger is to live at a diminished capacity. Even mild degrees of emotional upset affect our thinking, feelings and behavior. The more severe our anger, the more severely we are affected.

To live at optimal capacity, we must assume responsibility for freeing ourselves from the shackles of hate, anger, and hurt. These shackles not only restrict our freedom, they restrict our personal identities. They lower our standards and diminish our accomplishments. Most of us do not even like ourselves when we are angry. Others do not like us either.

Fortunately, we can free ourselves from these cruel shackles. Forgiveness is a key available to each of us at all times.

28

"The art of being able to make good use of moderate abilities wins esteem, and often acquires more reputation than actual brilliancy."

—Frances Rouchefoucauld

Someone once commented, "God must have loved the common man because He made so many of them." Of course, most of us are ordinary people. Few of us will affect the course of world history or even be remembered beyond the span of our lives.

Yet, common people are important people. One brick in a wall is no less important than another. However, all of us are given special abilities and are responsible for how these abilities are used.

Forgiving does not take special ability. The ability to forgive is freely given to all; it is a much more important gift than brilliancy.

"Good temper, like a sunny day, sheds a brightness over everything. It is the sweetener of toil and soother of disquietude."

—Washington Irving

A forgiving spirit is contagious. People who practice forgiveness inspire others to forgive. People who forgive seem to permeate the atmosphere with love and assurance. They display a quality of life which extends beyond themselves and fills the environment with renewed hope.

Generally, we forgive people rather than circumstances. Yet, circumstances can easily produce an angry unforgiving spirit. An unforgiving spirit is also contagious and can quickly pollute the environment. Hostility is a perpetual storm cloud hanging over our lives.

When life circumstances seem unbearable, remember, how *long* we live is not as important as how *well* we live. Forgiving people usually leave the world brighter and sunnier than they found it.

"I am part of all that I have met."

—Alfred Tennyson

We are not only influenced by those we meet, those we meet are also influenced by meeting us. Learning, growth, and development are largely accomplished through various forms of human interaction. Knowledge and wisdom are developed by exchanging information and experiences.

People who forgive seem to have the ability to give and receive the more noble qualities of human relationships. Forgiving people may encounter irritation but display patience; encounter anger but exhibit caring; encounter vengeance but manifest peace.

Meeting the right people is important. Being the right person is even more important. That part we leave with others may outlive us. Someone somewhere taught us the value of forgiveness.

"Principles are very important, but they need to be adorned by the graces to render them attractive."

—Anonymous

The idea of forgiveness is not very attractive. People who forgive are beautiful. To read about forgiveness may be interesting at best. To meet a forgiving person is encouraging. To behold forgiving people actually practice forgiveness is inspiration.

Many sermons are preached on the virtues of forgiveness. Most of these sermons are effective only as long as the posterior endurance of those who hear them can be maintained. We may even breathe a sigh of relief when the last "Amen" is pronounced.

Forgiveness removes emotional and spiritual bitterness. An old saying and popular song ventures, "A spoonful of sugar makes the medicine go down." People who practice forgiveness help us understand that even massive doses of forgiveness are palatable, even desirable.

AUGUST

"Ability is a poor man's wealth."

—M. Wren, *Sunrise to Starlight*

Few of us are endowed with natural abilities. Abilities must be learned, practiced, refined, and applied. Some abilities require a lifetime to master. These are the abilities most admired, but are usually the least developed.

Fortunately, a lack of monetary resources does not restrict our wealth of forgiveness. The ability to forgive provides a reservoir of wealth beyond the scope of Wall Street.

The ability to forgive others is an investment which pays attractive dividends. Like any other investment, there are risks. We need to carefully manage our forgiveness portfolios. Our forgiveness may be rejected. Desired reconciliations may fail. We may become discouraged. However, forgiveness tends to be a very sound investment in our own character development, relationships with others, and personal happiness.

2 *Learning to Forgive Rejection*

The hurt of rejection is one of the most devastating injuries a person can experience. In bereavement, we may feel a loved one has rejected or abandoned us. Children who suffer emotional or physical rejection are often damaged for life. They withhold trust, fearing they will be hurt again. Some become unable to feel love. Adults react in much the same way.

Forgiving rejection is not easy; we must first deal with excruciating pain. But the sooner we are able to forgive rejection, the sooner the healing process can begin.

Dr. Glenn Doman, noted authority on teaching children to read, discovered some children who have had as much as half of their brains surgically removed could still be taught to read. If these children can learn to read, surely we can learn to forgive.

Warning: Responsibility Can Be Hazardous to Your Health

Assuming responsibility for mending damage caused by the misconduct of others is unfair. We may feel unable to control our lives and circumstances. Like children, we are apt to give up in shame.

But giving up indicates immaturity, not inability. Toddlers may revert to crawling after a fall, but eventually find walking a better way of locomotion.

Risk is a part of life. We do not love without risk of hurt and rejection. Routinely, we calculate those hazards that are worthwhile. For instance, polio vaccines are not without chance. Yet, the majority of us will never again fear that crippling disease. Some risks—even serious ones—are acceptable. The risk of ongoing unrecognized emotional malignancy is not.

4 *Thank God for Guilt.*

We need not fear guilt. It is a natural though powerful experience. Too much guilt can stymie emotional maturity. Hospitals are full of people with too much guilt; jails are full of those with too little guilt.

To avoid guilt, some attempt to blame God or some other moral standard. But guilt is a personal experience; full responsibility rests with the individual. Many young people believe guilt is a disease the Puritans brought to America. Without morality, guilt has no meaning.

Guilt has an important purpose; it regulates behavior. Without guilt we would never feel the need to forgive ourselves and get better. Self-forgiveness is the only cure for guilt. Thank God for healthy guilt; it keeps us between the ditches.

"Impossibilities recede as experience advances."

—Arthur Helps, *Friends in Council*

Heavier than air flight seemed impossible until the Wright brothers dumbfounded the world by demonstrating flight at Kitty Hawk, North Carolina. Each experiment provided the Wright brothers with new information and levels of experience. Finally the impossibility of flight receded into reality.

Experience in aviation continued to develop. Still, transatlantic flight seemed impossible until Charles Lindbergh gained enough experience to fly across the Atlantic. Another "impossibility" fell to accomplishment.

Without experience, forgiveness may seem impossible. Yet, with each endeavor to forgive, we gain experience. We learn by experience that some impossibilities may not be impossible after all.

6

"May the outward and the inward man be at one."

—Socrates

Most of us get out of balance from time to time. We become confused about our feelings and seem incapable of regaining our equilibrium or knowing what to do. We struggle to reconcile the past or plan for the future.

One cause for such disorientation is that we are out of sync with ourselves. We know the difference between right and wrong but contradict our own values. In an effort to put our lives back into balance, we may debunk our values and become even more unstable.

For example, teenagers complain values are "old-fashioned." In truth, real values are more than "old fashioned," they are "ancient."

Forgiving ourselves when we are out of sync is an honest means of regaining our balance. Though we may experience a new sense of inner peace, the idea is as old as Socrates.

"Cheer up; it could be worse."

Sometimes bad things seem to happen all at once. Some believe bad occurrences come in threes. Two hard luck situations foreshadow a third.

Truly, life can be perplexing. Grief, financial reverses, school problems, marital difficulties, parenting concerns, and broken hearts are just a few predicaments that typically besiege us.

"Cheer up, it could be worse," is an effort to be comforting. Like Job, we find little comfort in such advice. Someone once commented, "I cheered up and sure enough things got worse." A teenager whose girlfriend rejected him when he lost his driver's license summarized, "Life stinks."

Of course, we cannot always control adverse circumstances. At such times, can things get worse? Indeed they can. What if we should become bitter and lose our ability to love, care, and forgive!

"I don't even know what it was about."

Three months after a suicide attempt a young lady, seventeen, recalled being angry at her father. She also recalled forgiving him and reconciling their relationship. When questioned further, she stated, "I don't even know what it was about."

Time has a way of erasing many of our hurts, anger, anxieties, and stresses. Forgiveness tempered with time helps us make healthy resolutions.

Forgiveness allows time to alter the intensity of our feelings which helps us gain a more realistic perception. Intense anger today may not seem so important tomorrow. Sometimes, raw anger seems louder and more intense than the actual situation.

Anger, hurt, and frustrations are seldom permanent. Suicide is permanent. For this fortunate young lady, forgiveness healed her soul and saved her life.

Guilty for Feeling Guilty

A lady once said, "I'm guilty if I'm late; I'm guilty if I drive too fast." Most of us can identify with the feeling. Guilt is healthy until it runs amok.

As children, shame and guilt brought a sense of security. We felt safe when someone else told us how we should feel. This was particularly valuable when life was in chaos.

As adults, we are driven by these winds of shame and guilt as we navigate through life. When parents no longer manipulate us, we search for others to take over the job. Without shame and guilt we may feel becalmed at sea—stranded.

No one can mash our guilt buttons unless we permit it. Yet, to forgive those who have ruthlessly controlled our guilt is to risk living without steerage. First, we must forgive ourselves for allowing them to assume command.

10 *"If needless guilt helped, I'd be perfect."*

Needless guilt is guilt bereft of reason. It becomes self-destructive. We experience anger toward ourselves and this, in turn, produces more guilt. We have successfully achieved perpetual motion.

Suicidal people, caught up in needless guilt, see no way out—no hope for relief. They believe no one cares and they, therefore, cannot accept caring. Having learned to hate themselves, they cannot accept love from others.

There is no therapeutic value in needless self-blame. Undeserved self-recrimination has no virtue. Self-forgiveness is the only antidote for guilt. To overcome needless guilt without first forgiving self is like spitting into the wind.

An elderly man's wife threatened to leave him. She complained he was a tyrant, ruling the family with relentless rigidity. She offered two choices: become more flexible or live without her.

Searching his soul, he recalled how he had been abandoned by his mother. He never knew his father. An aunt tried for a while to support him, but she too abandoned him.

Late in life he realized his attempt to control his own family was based on the anger and hurt he had experienced as a child. After deep inward searching, he forgave his unwillingness to forgive as well as the years of his cruel behavior.

Forgiveness offers no guarantees other than inward peace. But in this case, the man salvaged his marriage and relationships with his own children and grandchildren. He learned late—but not too late.

12 *Keeping the Past in the Past*

To deny or distort the reality of our past is not healthy. Psychosis is basically separation from reality. To reshape the past is crazy. Bending reality may appear easier than forgiveness but is detrimental to our emotional, mental, and spiritual health.

To face the past may hurt. Confession to ourselves, others, or God is often beneficial.

Self-forgiveness involves a change in attitude toward ourselves. We no longer need to torture ourselves with cruel reminders of past misbehaviors that others have long forgotten. Instead, we learn from mistakes. Mistakes make good building material.

When we forgive our past, we no longer replay traumatic errors like worn-out movies. We no longer use the present to lament the past but to plan for the future.

Free at Last

No prisons are more confining than those we build for ourselves. Self-punishing behaviors range from rejecting compliments to involvement in destructive relationships, to drug or alcohol addiction, to suicide. All are symptoms of self-hate and self-imposed incarceration.

In forgiving ourselves, we issue our own Emancipation Proclamation. Healthy new attitudes emerge with personal freedoms and unfamiliar but exciting avenues of thinking, feeling, and behaving open up. Self-respect becomes a reality; it is no longer contingent on the approval of others.

Forgiveness frees us from the compulsion to judge ourselves harshly. We can now channel that energy into self-evaluation and personal growth.

Love Is for Sharing

Appropriate self-love is essential for personal maturity. A Biblical narrative comes to mind. A group of malcontents were arguing with Jesus when a lawyer stepped up and asked Him which is the most important commandment. The lawyer challenged Jesus to reduce volumes of laws written over centuries to a single statement. In reply, Jesus cited the ancient Shema teaching that one should love God with all their heart, soul, and mind. Then He offered an unsolicited second commandment: "You shall love your neighbor as yourself."

If we hate ourselves and love our neighbor in the same way, we are not likely to get along. If we are suicidal and love our neighbor in like manner, we might kill our neighbor. Worse yet, what if your neighbor hates himself?

Love is for sharing. Forgiving ourselves makes it meaningful.

Time for Action

Some of us grew up on old sayings such as, "Fish or cut bait" or "Take the bull by the horns" or perhaps, "It's time to get crackin.'" The message is the same. Nothing happens until we make it happen. Delay accomplishes nothing.

Marking a specific time can be helpful in our commitment to accomplish forgiveness. For instance, writing a detailed account of our anger and burning it with a ritual, may affirm our determination to get better. Some ceremonies may be traditional or uniquely personal. They are not magic but they mark symbolically that point when forgiveness was born.

The most common temptation is to put the need to forgive on hold. Excuses abound but decisive action ends the delay that perpetuates the hurt. Healing begins when forgiveness takes place.

Naomi, aka Mara

The case of Naomi, also known as Mara, may be one of the most vivid descriptions ever recorded of the contrast between bitterness and betterness. Naomi's experiences, found in the biblical Book of Ruth, could prove helpful when we feel defeated.

Drought forced Naomi and her husband to move to Moab where her husband and both her married sons died, leaving three destitute widows. One daughter-in-law returned to her family. Naomi and Ruth were left alone.

Naomi, accompanied by Ruth, returned to Bethlehem. As friends greeted Naomi (meaning pleasant) she insisted they call her Mara (meaning bitter).

The depth of her agony and eventual recovery has inspired many for centuries.

Use the Old Brain Stem

It takes more than one heroic episode to become a forgiving person. Each episode is a step in the right direction. Sustained emotional and physical health comes when we incorporate forgiveness into our personalities.

A function of the brain stem is to take over repetitive tasks. For example, learning to pedal a bicycle or learning to walk and chew gum at the same time. Once these skills are mastered, we are likely to retain them for the rest of our lives.

To live as a forgiving person requires practice and energy. Eventually, forgiveness becomes more unrehearsed. This is also true for being hateful and bitter. The difference? Bitterness is an emotional disease which weakens. Forgiveness, on the other hand, is constructive and builds strength.

18 *Forgiving, Healing, and Growing*

The quest for improvement is consistent with human history. Personal hygiene would have meant very little to our primitive ancestors. Bad breath, body odor, and dandruff were not vital issues. Even toilet paper was not introduced until the 1880's.

Today's modern populace enjoys improved health and life through these and other social customs. We have achieved these improvements largely by building onto basic social laws that have stood the test of time and proved to be essential to civilized living—the value of human life, for instance.

Forgiveness is a time-honored law which provides a foundation for emotional, spiritual, and social stability. We attain healing and growth by building onto forgiveness. This is no less important to our total development than soap, toothpaste, and toilet paper.

Now and then we are helpless to change a painful situation. One man, extremely frustrated by his boss, said, "It's hard to forgive an ignoramus who will always be an ignoramus."

Instinctive reactions toward someone who perpetually hurts us is natural and does not necessarily indicate we have failed to forgive. Keep in mind, healing may take longer than forgiving. This is especially true when someone mistreats us who has a vested interest in our agony or humiliation.

How long or how many times should we forgive? Is seventy times seven enough? Should we keep score so that after the 490th offense we can finally break their face? The real question is, how much forgiveness is needed to get better and stay that way? Indeed, forgiveness is very personal.

How far is far enough?

What is forgivable and what is not forgivable is an inevitable question—and a reasonable one, but in the wrong direction. The real question asks what are we willing to forgive; how far are we willing to go to forgive?

Only we can set those limits. Nothing is unforgivable unless we make it so. Although hatred may win the support of others, the emotional disease is locked inside and the damage continues. No rules declare that we cannot go beyond human limitations. Our commitment to forgive, then, should be no less limited.

How far is far enough? It is far enough when we are finally able to forgive, heal, and grow.

Nonforgiveness: Giving Up, Going Down, in Defeat

An adolescent boy had lived in institutions for many years. He was not delinquent, mentally ill, unattractive, or stupid. He was the son of heroin-addicted parents whom he blamed and felt unable to forgive.

Nonforgiveness may be defined as simply a refusal to forgive. Some variations include:

"I will hate her 'til the day I die."

"I will never forgive my father."

" I can't (won't) forgive!"

Nonforgiveness comes in two forms. *Specific* nonforgiveness pertains to feelings toward a particular individual and may be related to one or more offense. *Pervasive* nonforgiveness is an unwillingness to forgive anyone; it effectively blocks all channels for emotional or spiritual healing and growth. Nonforgiveness is a crash and burn approach to getting better.

22

"The infliction of cruelty with a good conscience is a delight to moralists. That's why they invented hell."

—Bertrand Russell

Pseudo-forgiveness is easy to define but difficult to identify since counterfeit forms of forgiveness appear genuine. Some examples include:

"I'll forgive but I'll never forget."

"I'll forgive but make sure it never happens again."

"I'll forgive but I pray God will make him suffer as much as I have."

When Frederick William I, King of Prussia (1713-40), was dying, the queen advised he forgive his brother-in-law, George II of England. The king ordered her to write her brother and tell him he was forgiven. "But," he said, "do not do it until I am dead."

Pseudo-forgiveness often disguises bitterness. Ironically, it can mask hostility making it look like a virtue.

Conditional Forgiveness: A Good Try With Mixed Results

Conditional forgiveness is easy to define and not particularly difficult to practice. Simply defined, conditional forgiveness is, "I will forgive if (when)..." Add any condition expected of the offender:

"I'll forgive if she says she is sorry."

"I'll forgive if he pays for it."

"I forgive when he stops mistreating me."

Conditional forgiveness works at times. However, our inner peace is at the mercy of the offender. If our conditions are met, we get better; if they are not met, we are left in our own anger. Heinrich Heine (1797-1856) reflected the attitude of conditional forgiveness, "We should forgive our enemies, but only after they have been hanged."

True forgiveness need not be in the hands of an offender.

24 *The Golden Pinnacle: Unconditional Forgiveness*

The epitome of unconditional forgiveness was demonstrated centuries ago. It altered the entire course of human history. Under a blistering sun, Jesus of Nazareth was nailed to a cross and died in naked humiliation. Gamblers rolled dice for His robe; His dignity was crushed. He was the victim of cold-blooded, calculated slaughter. When one is robbed of life, all else pales into insignificance. No one can perpetrate a greater crime.

Yet, at the height of excruciating pain and depth of despair, He cried out, "Father, forgive them; they know not what they do." His forgiveness did not require the return of his robe, a change of heart among those cruel people, or that they spare His life. Without conditions, He simply forgave.

"For I know my transgressions and my sin is ever before me."

–Psalm 51

Our faith tells us God is the kind of Friend who will listen to our anger—and listen to our pleas to curb it, understand it, express it, get beyond it. Change the following "prayer-words" into your words, as you speak to your loving Friend:

Dear God, You already know what I'm angry about, just as any good friend knows when we're angry even though we may try not to show it. Listen to me, Lord, as my Friend who wants to know every little detail and who responds to me with the simple words, "How can I help?"

"In her bruised and unforgiving way, Maggie did love her elder sister. But it was family-style love, the kind that starts off flowing like a river and then builds up a lot of sediment."

—Indiana Gothic

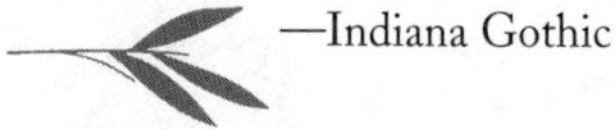

In families, nothing says forgiveness like forgiving. When married couples have a bone to pick, and their kids see them discussing the situation calmly—and making up—this sets a great example. And we mustn't be afraid to tell our children we are sorry when we have hurt them. Parents aren't always "automatically right" or somehow "above" apologizing to their children. Telling a child of one's sorrow and repentance and asking forgiveness doesn't undermine our authority. Rather, it lets our children see that we are human, we make mistakes, and that we can do the right thing to make amends.

"Just pick it up and say hello."

—Michael, age 14

Several years ago my family and I were driving through the mountains of Colorado in my brother-in-law's very nice recreational vehicle. It had one of those (at that time) new-fangled car phones mounted on the console, with all kinds of buttons everywhere.

My young son, Michael, was riding in the front seat with me when the phone rang. Not knowing just what to do, I panicked and turned to my techno-son with the question: "What do I DO with this thing?!" His simple, calm answer: "Just pick it up and say hello!"

It worked. Sometimes we want to over-complicate things…things like forgiveness. Maybe the simple, easy way is the right way. Maybe we just need to pick up the phone and say hello.

28

"For me, this was liberation."

—Rev. Joseph A. Bradley, quoted in a CareNote

For the first five days after his wife's death, Rev. Bradley didn't cry, because he was so preoccupied with fulfilling responsibilities and expectations. "As a result," he recalls, "my tear ducts got all plugged up and my eyes became infected. My eye infection was a reminder...to cry freely. People could walk by me and look at me crying, and it really didn't make any difference to me. For me, this was liberation."

We need to "liberate" ourselves from anger and non-forgiveness just as much as from grief. But instead of (or in addition to) crying freely, we need to know we may pray freely.

"Lord, create in me a love for peace: not peace that is the absence of struggle, nor peace that is blind to injustice, but peace that makes whole what now is broken."

—Further Everyday Prayers

Ask for divine help in your struggle to forgive. The God of the Judeo-Christian tradition has an ancient reputation for compassion and mercy. Try praying for your enemy. Don't just ask for a change in that person's heart or behavior; really pray for him or her. You may find it hard to find words for such a prayer, but words are not necessary to the God who knows your mind and heart. Just stand before God with that person at your side, and let God's love wash over both of you until it penetrates your heart.

30 *"I'm free; I'm totally free."*

—Answer to "How do you feel?" given by an old man after forgiving another and himself

Forgiving is possible. Not easily, not quickly, perhaps, but you can free yourself from the memory which brings such bitter sorrow—and, in the process, heal the wound that has throbbed so long. We must remember that forgiving is not a moment of tear-streaked reunion and peace; it is a process, a journey of the heart.

There is no jet-service to forgiveness and freedom and peace. No rocket can hurdle you to the journey's end. But with patience and perseverance, you can find the peace you seek.

"Forgive them, Father! They don't know what they're doing."

—From Luke 23

We need not feel obligated to make excuses for the person who hurt us. Excusing and forgiving are not the same thing. We may excuse the small child who spills the too-full glass of milk; but we must forgive the grown child who turns against us.

The challenge is to come to some understanding, to the best of our ability, of what was going on inside the offender. And then, once we have a clearer picture of what happened and why, we face the moment of real decision: Do we really want to forgive?

SEPTEMBER

"Forgiveness is giving up all hope for a better past."

—Anonymous

We need to forgive so that we can move forward with life. An unforgiven injury binds us to a time and place someone else has chosen; it holds us trapped in a past moment and in old feelings. Forgiveness is our ticket to freedom. Write down what difference forgiving will make in your life. What will you gain—and what will you lose?

Are you willing to lose the company of your dark feelings? Have you the courage to step out into the future without carrying the all-too-familiar weight?

2

"My own heart let me more have pity on."

—Gerard Manley Hopkins

Someone has said that the sins of all humanity are but a single hot coal in the ocean of God's mercy. Wouldn't it be wonderful if our own mercy were so deep and vast that an injury against us would just make a tiny kerplunk in our souls? But we are not God, and the injuries we suffer can send out wave after wave of hurt.

Nevertheless, it is possible, through the grace of God, to forgive. There is even a bonus: When we forgive, we both give and we get.

"We all need to summon the courage to be imperfect."

—Alfred Adler, psychologist

Think about the people you love and admire most and say a little prayer for them. How do they handle their anger? Pray to be more like them in this regard. Pray for the ability to accept situations where a loved one's anger—and your own—are justified.

If it is a loved one you are angry with and are having a hard time forgiving, remember how writer Lawrence Crabb, Jr., defines marriage: "Any marriage is the union of two sinners. A happy marriage is the union of two forgivers."

Finally, pray for the wisdom to allow yourself and others to express negative feelings without attacking and turning into a "monster."

4

"We cannot do it alone. The good news is that we don't have to."

—Lambert Reilly, O.S.B.

When it comes to forgiveness, we don't have it within ourselves to bring it off, and we know that. But, fortunately, this is why we have God, the church, community, sacraments, rituals, the Word of God, the encouragement and the accountability that come with being a member of a faith community, a child of God. May the following prayer help you draw strength from these blessings:

God, help me to see with an inner vision. Help me to see beyond facades and masks to the inner world of those I know. Help me to find there the flawed beauty of those in need of renewal and wholeness. O God, help me to know my own flaws, the hidden places that I try to hide from others and myself, and from you. Amen.

"A chip on the shoulder indicates there is wood higher up."

—Jack Herbert

Another way of stating this is that much-despised piece of advice, "Don't take it personally." Or, as a paraphrase of a proverb puts it: "It's not raining on you; it's just raining."

Oftentimes we can reduce our anger and frustration levels by letting go of unrealistic expectations—of ourselves, of others, of the world we live in.

"Life is difficult" is the first line of the best-selling book, *The Road Less Traveled.* The fact that this book could be honest and real helped it speak effectively to millions of readers.

6 *"Dad's memory is failing—but that doesn't keep him from remembering a grudge."*

—Anonymous

We all need love the most when we are the most unlovable! When we act out in anger, we "blow it," and say or do something we come to regret, we need to work on forgiveness. We need to ask for it. And we need to work on forgiving ourselves, too.

In everyone's life there are events for which we need to forgive ourselves. But there may also be events which we have wrongly ascribed the guilt of others to our own faults and weaknesses.

Let this prayer guide your reflection:

Dear God, help me to understand anger I may have toward myself. Help me to overcome feelings of shame and inadequacy. Touch my life today with the reassurance of your presence, of your acceptance and your wonder. Amen.

"I have learned that harboring resentment is like drinking a cup of poison and expecting the other person to die."

—Member of a 12-step recovery group

Did you know that Saint Patrick was kidnapped from England and sold as a slave in Ireland? Think of the incredible forgiveness he portrayed in his life by eventually going back to Ireland and working successfully to bring the faith to his former "owners."

8

"If I can hear only what I already know, I can never learn anything new."

—Bernard Lonergan, S.J.

We have to go out of our way and pay special attention to listen carefully. This is the only way to break out of our habitual ways of thinking. When we think of a "transgressor," we can often hear ourselves say, "Well, you know how HE is."

When we listen anew—or for the first time—that doesn't mean we are going to agree with what we hear. Far from it. But it may give us some understanding we never had before. It keeps us at least open to the possibility that when we hear the other person's viewpoint or see his/her vantage point, we may be changed ourselves, gaining new insights into our very selves.

"Every day is Saturday to a dog."

—Roger Miller

Yes, dogs get angry—very angry. But more often in our world of domesticated animals (pets), we come to know dogs that are loyal, laid-back, slow to anger and quick to forgive.

What do dogs know that we don't know? (Or what don't they know that we do know?!) They seem to take life in stride, living in the moment, sort of like we did back when we were small and not so much in need of always needing to not only know what was going to happen next but to be in charge and control of what is going to happen next! Let the following begin your prayer: Dear God, Help me realize that "every day can be Saturday" for me, too, knowing and believing deeply in your love and protection and guidance. Help me see the freedom and peace that trust in you can bring.

10 *"Love means to love that which is unlovable, or it is no virtue at all; forgiving means to pardon that which is unpardonable, or it is no virtue at all—and to hope means hoping when things are hopeless, or it is no virtue at all."*

—G.K. Chesterton

Being human, we may never be able to feel totally loved, totally secure—so secure in love that nothing will ever feel like a threat to us; and nothing will then make us angry. But we can, through prayer, work at reducing our insecurities.

We are safe and secure, our faith teaches us, only in God's love. Pause for a few minutes and try to think of only one thing: God's love. How can this faith in God's love make you more yourself, more alive, more forgiving, and more at peace?

"It's difficult to make peace with your anger if you view it as your enemy."
—Tom McGrath, "Making Peace With Anger"

Part of the spirituality of being a mature adult is, in the words of the great philosopher Kenny Rogers, knowing "when to hold 'em, when to fold 'em, and when to walk away." Sometimes the best thing to do with your anger is just to drop it. But in order to drop it, you first have to take hold of your anger and see it for what it is. It's not your enemy.

Reflect on the following quote from the great Greek philosopher, Aristotle: "Anybody can become angry; that is easy. But to be angry with the right person, and to the right degree, and at the right time, and for the right purpose, and in the right way—that is not within everybody's power and is not easy."

12

"I live through the mercy of Jesus, to whom I owe everything and from whom I expect everything."

—Pope John XXIII

Forgiveness doesn't come naturally. We can't get very far without divine help. Perhaps the single most important and helpful activity is prayer—prayer for oneself to be able to forgive, and prayer for the other person (trying to avoid harsh sentiments like, "Help him not be such a jerk!"). When we pray, we need only wait to witness the spiritual transformation God can work.

"Who can detect failings? From hidden faults forgive me."

—Psalm 19

With me it's usually not "hidden." I can mislead myself for a while, or be mislead by others for a while, and then the wicked truth comes home: It's up to me here to make a move.

At first, laying the blame at another's feet, or waiting for them to make the first move, seems to be the right answer. But when we slip into a blaming pattern, we are unable to take control even when we may want to. Blaming keeps us from taking responsibility. It's a surrender of the power to change our lives for the better.

14

"On the royal road to Thebes
I had my luck,
I met a lovely monster,
And the story's this:
I made the monster me."

—Stanley Kunitz, The Approach to Thebes

The best horror stories are about someone familiar, someone "good," turning into a monster: Jekkyl and Hyde, The Body Snatchers, etc. It really shouldn't surprise us that the people we know and love can hurt us the most—and we in turn, can hurt most the people we know.

Anger can destroy not only the people around us, but it can become a monster that eats at our very souls. How can we achieve success in mastering this powerful emotion?

If I can't forget, can I still forgive?

Some people claim they can forgive and forget. These individuals gladly recite a menu of injuries they have forgotten. Realistically, the ability to forget is an illusive quality. We may find ourselves caught between our desire to forgive and our inability to forget.

Forgetting is an attempt to disarm anger, to terminate all hope or need to retaliate. To disarm the potency of hostility is an essential part of forgiveness. Disarming is possible; forgetting is not. However, memory cannot refire hatred unless we allow it to do so.

To disarm outrage requires a few basic internal commitments. To disarm effectively, we must make a firm decision to bury our hatred; refuse to resurrect it; determine never to use it against the offender; forfeit our right to vengeance; and finally, continue living and growing as if we had never been injured.

16 *"Usually the area in life in which we are the most defensive in ourselves is the area we are least tolerant of in others."*

—Anonymous

Just as God gives you anger to protect yourself, God provides courage to take the positive action your anger demands. Your courage is within you; ask God to help you find it.

Is your anger a call from God to change? A call from God to do something? Something only you can do? Say a prayer for wisdom and guidance and courage as you discern what God may be telling you.

"Why do you treat your servant so badly?...Why are you so displeased with me that you burden me with all this people?"

—Moses, in Numbers 11:11-12

Scripture is filled with the stories of countless holy folks who expressed their indignation at God. And all of us can identify at some time or another with the psalmist who cries out, "How long, O Lord? Will you utterly forget me? How long will you hide your face from me?" (13:2).

In our prayer, we turn to God in complete confidence that God can right what has gone wrong, that God expects us not to suffer in silence but to raise our voices and ask God to hear our cries.

18 *"Lord Thou madest us for Thyself, and we can find no rest till we find rest in Thee."*

—St. Augustine

Human beings are a unique creation. In many ways we are allowed to be co-creators of ourselves. We are given life, potential, and an inner moral compass. Finally we are given responsibility for using these basic tools of life.

Love appears to be our moral compass; forgiveness points the way. When hatred alters our course our potential is diminished or lost. Anger, rage, depression, and frustration are deeply disturbing. Our lives become disrupted; we find no rest.

Forgiveness puts us back into balance. By forgiving others we synchronize ourselves with God's design. When we forgive, we too affirm, "Lord Thou madest us for Thyself, and we can find no rest till we find rest in Thee."

"The greatest fault is to be conscious of none."

—Thomas Carlyle

Take a prayer-walk. Take along with you your list of worries, your fears, your sadnesses, the things that cause you anger. Drop them off, one by one, as you walk with God at your side.

As you walk, make a prayer of this provocative conclusion from the diaries of holocaust victim, Etty Hilessum: "It is the only thing we can do....[we] must turn inwards and destroy in ourselves all that we think we ought to destroy in others."

20

"I like things done my own special way...and by someone else."

—*New Yorker* cartoon

We want the car in front of us to be traveling at the exact speed we want to be traveling—not slower, for certain. If not, we get angry. Being selfish creatures, we want things to go our way. The healthy thing to do with our anger is to be selfish about it, too! We need to make "I" statements to people, so that we can locate the blame where it belongs—inside of us. People are not responsible for your anger, only for their actions. No one else can "make" you angry, and no one else can take your anger away.

What "I" statements can you make to God about the anger you feel?

"My husband and I have accepted each other in our imperfection. Amazingly, that has eliminated all my rage and frustration."

—Anonymous

Some of us get enslaved to the past and pain and burn with resentment, anger, even bitterness. We just can't seem to let go. But for those who can let go, who can forgive, it's a beautiful thing to see and hear about.

And often it is the smallest of things (or an accumulation of small things) which are hardest to forgive. After all, life is so full of "the small stuff"—especially our lives with the people we spend the most time with.

22

"Sinners cannot find God for the same reason that criminals cannot find a policeman: They aren't looking!"

—Billy Sunday

Pick up a newspaper, and look at all the headlines that report the terror and anger and desperation in our world. Then pray for your sisters and brothers everywhere:

Dear Lord, I know firsthand that anger can be a painful emotion—a powerful emotion that can leave us feeling helpless, defeated, paralyzed. But I also know that you stand ready to help us release and resolve our anger peacefully.

"If you, O Lord, mark iniquities,
Lord, who can stand?
But with you is forgiveness,
That you may be revered."

—Psalm 130

In a tale from Jewish folklore, a believer addresses God on the eve of Yom Kippur, Israel's annual celebration of human repentance. He recites to God the great suffering endured by virtuous members of his community. And he offers a deal: "If you forgive us, we will forgive you." God constantly holds out forgiveness to us. Now and then we have to return the favor. And making up, they say, is the sweetest part of a lovers' quarrel.

24

"The Bible says God is slow to anger. That's a trait worth imitating. When you're angry, slow down."

—Tom McGrath, *Making Peace With Anger*

In the midst of anger, we often speak or act impulsively. Everything seems very urgent. Yet very few situations demand a decision or response this very moment. Slowing down helps us disengage a bit and stay calm. Venting anger just to be venting rarely brings lasting change. Remaining calm, while continuing to assert your needs, is the more likely way to bring about long-term change.

Letting go of anger often means finding the way to forgive. Use these lines from the Lord's prayer to help you: "Forgive us our trespasses as we forgive those who trespass against us." It takes grace to forgive and be free. Ask God for that grace—and freedom.

"Mea culpa, mea culpa, mea maxima culpa."

—from the pre-Vatican II
Roman Catholic Mass

Reflect on these unconventional prayer-insights written by Etty Hillesum: "And if God does not help me to go on, then I shall have to help God."

"Yes, we carry everything within us, God and Heaven and Hell...and Life and Death....And we have to take everything that comes: the bad with the good, which does not mean we cannot devote our life to curing the bad. But we must know what motives inspire our struggle and we must begin with ourselves, every day anew."

26

"God is not nice. God is not an uncle. God is a volcano."

—Hasidic saying

Even if there seems to be no good answer to such a question as, "How can a good God let this terrible thing happen?", it's still a question worth asking when we are angry at some unfairness. By struggling with and facing realities, and especially by entering into mystery, we grow spiritually.

As Christians we believe that God wants to be in relationship with us no matter what we are feeling. God stands at the door ready to help us overcome the pain of this world. Say a short prayer that your anger will not become so all-consuming that you will not hear God knocking at your door.

Invite God inside your home and shout all the reasons you are angry. Ask God to hold your anger for you.

"And Satan trembles when he sees,
The weakest saint upon his knees."
—William Cowper

We need a time in our lives when we can say, "I am sorry" and a time when we can say, "You are forgiven." There might be tense relationships in families, between friends, with co-workers or neighbors. There might be old hurts and pains that need to be cured. We may even need to be reconciled with the past, with memories, with ourselves, or with God. Is this the time for a jubilee? Certainly! Sound the trumpet throughout all the land and let the celebration begin!

In what ways can I celebrate forgiveness? Lord, Open my heart to the spirit of celebration! Give me generosity of mind and soul that I might do what is necessary to seek the fullness of life in you.

28

"He who deliberates fully before taking a step will spend his entire life on one leg."

—Chinese Proverb

One myth we frequently struggle with is the persistent myth of happiness. Many times we are led to believe that we are supposed to be happy and fulfilled all of the time. We believe that it is our right to have possessions, love, respect and we feel inadequate if we do not have what everyone on television seems to have. Of course, this is a problem because our vision of happiness and success might be skewed or we fail to realize that all real rewards come with real costs. We can only be truly fulfilled when we realize that struggle and striving are also a natural part of life.

We do well to pray: Lord, help me to embrace my struggles and disappointments as something that will lead me farther down the road of life to true fulfillment and understanding of your will in my life.

"Not So Much to Be Understood as to Understand"

—St. Francis of Assisi

Even though the St. Francis Peace Prayer has us praying, "Lord, I pray not so much to be understood as to understand," we human beings long to be understood. We can get quite angry when we're not understood. As a matter of fact, it is often people's ignorance, apathy, inertia which drive us the maddest.

We all know the feeling of being walked away from, ignored, given "the silent treatment," or having someone pretend there is nothing wrong. Pray along with the Peace Prayer of St. Francis:

Lord, make me an instrument of your peace.

Where there is hatred, let me sow your love.

Where there is injury, your pardon, Lord.

30

"The strongest principle of growth lies in human choice."

—George Eliot

Lesson: You can choose to forgive.

"But what about my right to be angry?" And, while we're at it: "Is it fair to let the person who caused me harm to get away with it?" Most of us know in our hearts that forgiving someone is the right thing to do—but it's not something we so readily feel like doing.

Let the following African schoolgirl's prayer be your own prayer of forgiveness: "O thou great Chief, light a candle in my heart, that I may see what is therein and sweep the rubbish from thy dwelling place."

October

We need "a holy anger…which moves us to reprove with warmth those our mildness failed to correct."

—St. Jean Baptiste de la Salle

In his life, Jesus was known for both his gentleness and for his holy anger. In Jerusalem, the Holy City, Jesus came face to face with the crass and greedy money-changers in the temple. It pained him that they conducted their corrupt business in such a holy place, and he expressed his anger forcefully, driving them out of the temple. Jesus demonstrated how we can summon righteous anger in the cause of good. How we can "be angry…but not sin."

Make today's prayer a simple question: "What would you do, Jesus, about………?"

2 *"Always we begin again."*

—Benedictine tenet

The Benedictine monks, who have been "working at it" now for over 1500 years, live by the slogan, "Always we begin again." Oftentimes the Christian journey may seem like the taking of two steps backward for each step forward. And yet, it is only self-forgiveness that allows for forward movement. If we keep "dwelling" on our past mistakes, the past will become our "dwelling-place."

After we move ourselves out of this stagnant place, we can move toward the even larger challenge which Martin Luther posed so bluntly to all who would forgive the past and its many transgressions: "To do so no more is the truest repentance."

"Self-forgiveness cleanses the soul, washing away shame and guilt. Out of self-forgiveness comes the power to extend forgiveness to others."

—Forgiveness Therapy

Forgiving ourselves lifts a burden which gives us an appreciation for the merit of forgiving others. No one can know the inner recesses of our souls as well as we ourselves know them. No one can read our minds, or fully comprehend our feelings. No one can fully appreciate the lifting of shame and guilt we experience when we extend to ourselves the grace of self-forgiveness.

Indeed, forgiving ourselves is a very private experience. Yet, forgiving ourselves equips us to forgive others. Both forgiving ourselves and forgiving others take place within the confines of our hearts. Both types of forgiveness are processed in the same crucible. Forgiving others includes the hope they too will experience cleansing and freedom from the shackles of shame and guilt which restricted our own souls.

4

"Hanging on to old anger is like clutching a burning coal."

—Harriet Goldhor Lerner

The author of *The Dance of Anger,* Harriet Goldhor Lerner, compares hanging on to old anger to clutching a burning coal. Unless we express our anger in ways that lead to real change in our lives, we will be holding on to an emotion that may be burning a hole in our heart.

It is infuriating to have one's anger ignored by another. And yet we try so often to ignore our own anger—especially "old," lingering anger—the pain of our past. God can help us heal that pain—today.

Because for God, time is irrelevant. And even for us humans, the only time we have left is now and tomorrow.

"Nothing on earth consumes a man more quickly than the passion of resentment."

—Nietzche

If we are mad about something, chances are it is something important we are mad about, something important to us. Don't let anyone tell you "You shouldn't feel that way," "It's no big deal," or, "It's not the end of the world." God understands completely your feelings and wants to hear your side of the story.

Dear God: Give me the serenity to accept those things I cannot change, the courage to change the things I can, and the wisdom to know the difference.

6

"Every noble work is at first impossible."

—Thomas Carlyle

The pyramids appear impossible to build. Modern engineers can only theorize how they were built. Yet, after over 4000 years the pyramids stand as monuments to the impossible.

The fact a task appears impossible does not necessarily mean it cannot be done. Somehow the Egyptians found a way. Yet, to the Egyptians, travel to the moon would have seemed impossible. Even so, astronauts found a way.

Noble monuments or accomplishments are not completed easily. The pyramids were built a stone at a time. Lunar landers have been launched to the moon powered by huge rockets driven into space one stage at a time.

No doubt, forgiving others at times seems as formidable as building a pyramid or taking a journey to the moon. Impossible? Obviously not.

Some Christians believe that "true forgiveness is such a Divine quality that they don't have to practice it themselves."

—Garrison Keillor

Listen to one of the more expressive classical music composers, such as Mahler, Shostakovich, or Rachmaninoff. While listening, notice the dramatic rises and falls in the various movements, the fervent emotionalism and self-expression of the composers.

These artists felt deeply the highs and lows of life, the moments of deep serenity as well as outright rage. Even today, their compositions may rise up as prayers—as our prayers—as we let their notes and rhythms speak to God our feelings of anger, and our sincere wish to forgive and be forgiven.

8 *Character One: "I hate you, you.........!"*
Character Two: "Let's begin by defining your terms."

—Jules Feiffer cartoon

To affirm someone's anger, rather than to point the finger of blame, is a positive step in strengthening a relationship and in defusing anger. No one, after all, wants to have his or her anger disallowed. But dealing with anger directly, while an unpleasant and uncomfortable thing to do, can bring new learning and self-strengthening.

Dear Lord: Help me realize that it isn't necessary to agree with others in order to understand them. But also help me realize that it is impossible to truly agree without first understanding. Help me, Lord, be open to the possibility that when I hear another person's ideas I may even be changed myself!

"If you're waiting for justice, you're gonna wait a long time."

—Lambert Reilly, O.S.B.

Something in the human heart wants justice. Forgiving when repentance or reparation is lacking, when real reconciliation is perhaps impossible because of distance, death, or the other's unwillingness—that kind of forgiving rightfully outrages our sense of justice. We feel that some things don't, in decent human terms, deserve forgiveness.

But forgiving is not something you do for someone else. It is not even something you do because you should, according to the standards of religious belief or human decency. Forgiving is something you do for yourself. It is one way of becoming the person you were created to be—and fulfilling God's dream of you is the only way to true wholeness and happiness.

10

"My advice to all in relationships is the same as my advice to people who live in earthquake country: 'Don't dwell on faults.'"

—family therapist

Once you deal with your anger, you can turn your attention to forgiving. When you hold onto your resentment, you freeze yourself in the role of victim, freezing some of your emotional energy at the same time.

Let the warmth of understanding and the awareness of your worth thaw your emotions.

"Remember not the events of the past, the things of long ago consider not; See I am doing something new!"

—Isaiah 43, 18-19

To dwell on the past can be counterproductive. After all, there may have been situations or circumstances that you may not even know of or that were unavoidable. Or just plain stupid.

St. Augustine describes God as someone who "grows angry yet remains tranquil." I remember having a disciplinarian like that when I was a young boy in the seminary. Once a friend and I accidentally started a grass fire on the seminary grounds, playing with matches. I thought we would be expelled, decapitated, locked in church for two weeks. Instead, the disciplinarian, Father Kevin, remained tranquil in his anger, seeing the contrition in our eyes and shuddering knees.

12

"Be merciful to me, O God,
because of your constant love.
Because of your great mercy
Wipe away my sins!"

—Psalm 51

When we put all of this into God's hands, we find that the outcome is not in our hands, but in God's. And we are very different from God. We tend to want revenge, retaliation, the continuation of a grudge. But God has no desire to punish; instead God would rather show mercy. To overcome our resentments, we need nothing less than God's help. The good news is: It's there!

One more piece of good news: "God has set the right time for everything." (Ecclesiastes 3). That time just might be now!

"Anger is like fire. Fire is good when it keeps us warm and helps us cook food. But fire can sometimes get out of control."

—*Mad Isn't Bad*

Rev. Joseph W. Bradley was working as a public relations director at a medical center when his wife died five years ago. "Once I became so angry while at work that I went into the men's room and started punching a solid metal door. When I saw that I had hurt myself, I realized how stupid it was to do that." Six months later, when he became enraged at a supervisor for criticizing him unfairly, Bradley was able to express his anger in ways that were appropriate and empowering.

Do you find yourself hurting your own self sometimes—"pounding on a metal door"? Take a moment to think about what doors we need to OPEN instead of "punch at." Make a promise to yourself and to God to knock more often at God's door, especially in times of frustration, resentment, irritation.

14 *"God does not change what is in people until they change what is in themselves."*

—The Koran

It is good to remember that one of Christianity's greatest enemies, Saul of Tarsus, turned out to become one of the greatest witnesses to the good news of all time: St. Paul, apostle to the Gentiles. It was not only God's will that Paul convert from being a persecutor of Christians, it was God's will that he be seen as one changed by the spirit of God.

We can pray that those who have wronged us be changed as well, and that we be changed through a decision to forgive and to love.

"Failure always looks to the past. The future is now."

—from the movie, *The Hudsucker Proxy*

A friend tells the story of a woman who grew up in a home where arguments and punishment were the norm. Years later, she still resented her parents for the atmosphere they created. Her spiritual director encouraged the woman to ask her parents for forgiveness.

She decided only to ask her parents' pardon for resenting and blaming them for the way her life turned out. Both her father and mother were moved to tears by her humbleness and asked her forgiveness for being so harsh to her. They all felt as though a great burden had been lifted; the change was remarkable.

16

"We know we are sinners, but we also know we are forgiven. They go hand in hand."

—Matthew Kelty, O.C.S.O., Trappist monk

The Gospels tell us repeatedly that we are empowered to forgive one another only after we first allow God to overwhelm us with the gifts of gracious and merciful love. And, as with any gift, it takes a willing Giver and a willing receiver to be a real gift. Our God is a willing Giver. Are we willing receivers?

As St. Augustine puts it in his *Confessions:* "What indeed is more pitiful than a piteous person who has no pity for himself?"

"Forgiveness means canceling the charges against the other—and ourselves."

—Anthony G. Banet, Ph.D.

Being human has never been an easy task. Our humanity makes us vulnerable to heartbreak, disappointment, regret, and misdeeds. Our expectations of ourselves, along with the expectations others have for us, can be difficult or even impossible to meet sometimes.

By embracing our imperfections and limitations, however, we grow to accept ourselves as lovable children of God. We ease our sadness when we allow ourselves to make and learn from our human mistakes.

18 *"How unhappy is he who cannot forgive himself."*

—Publilius Syrus, *Moral Sayings*

"If only I had…I should have…Why didn't I?…" Sometimes the self-questioning can be quite maddening. We can question events and our responses to these events so much that we wonder how things could have been different. Sometimes we even take on guilt for things that were really beyond our control.

No one is perfect, and mistakes may have been made, but blaming ourselves for any tragedy in our life ultimately does nothing but weigh us down with unnecessary burdens. Recognize in the beginnings of self-forgiveness an important step in the journey to wholeness and healing.

"To forgive without compassion is not really forgiveness, just as a truce is not really peace. Real forgiveness understands the offender with love and compassion, not excusing the offense, but understanding the pain, the woundedness, from which almost every offense proceeds."

—John Garvey, "A God Who Hurts," *America*, Oct. 8, 1999

What is so surprising is not what people will not forgive, but what they will. Indeed, human beings have a powerful capacity to forgive and to grow.

20

"And it is glory to forgive the offense."
—Romans

So much of our anger is truly justifiable. And so many offenses seem unforgivable. While God doesn't demand that we have warm feelings toward all who have hurt us, God does ask us to "love our enemies" and "do good to those who hate us."

Love is sometimes described as an act of will rather than a matter of emotions. And thus loving our enemies is a matter of reining in our angry and bitter thoughts toward them, refusing to be mastered by resentment. It even means (and this is the tough part) consciously choosing to offer people goodness and kindness. Only God's help can bring us to such a high calling.

"Forgive me my sins, O Lord; forgive me the sins of my youth and the sins of mine age, the sins of my soul and the sins of my body, my secret and my whispering sins, my presumptuous and my crying sins, the sins I have done to please myself and the sins I have done to please others. Forgive me those sins which I know not; forgive them, O Lord, forgive them all of thy great goodness."

— *Private Devotions* (1560)

Unresolved guilt and remorse can cause sadness and even depression in our lives. And once depression takes hold, it's difficult to find the serenity to forgive ourselves and move on. But God understands our humanity and knows that our journeys through life will be sprinkled with mistakes and misjudgments. Prayer connects us with God's message of forgiveness, acceptance, and love. Prayer gives us strength and hope to begin again.

22

"Love your enemies and pray for those who persecute you."

—Matthew 5:44

"Praying for an enemy sounds like an easy out—and it is that if your prayer is really for yourself," writes Carol Luebering in her wonderful little book *The Forgiving Family: First Steps to Reconciliation*. "But when you stop praying for the other person's change of heart—for any kind of control over the other—and just pray for him or her, it's not easy at all. It's loving—and it will plunge you right into the heart of God.

"No one is safe, because the universe is hardly a safe place. It is often mean, unpredictable, and unjust. Loss has little to do with our notions of fairness."

—Jerry Sittser, *A Grace Disguised*

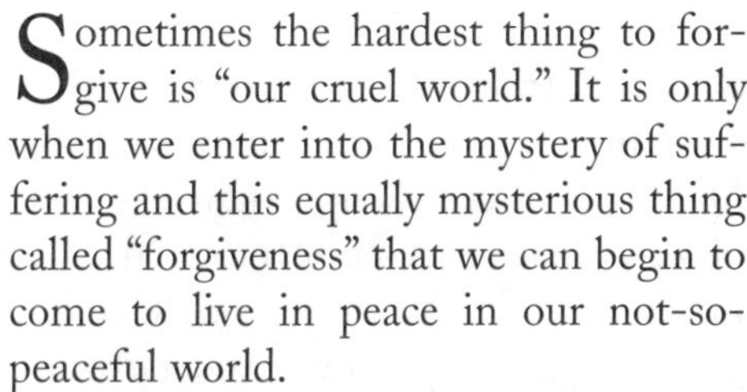

Sometimes the hardest thing to forgive is "our cruel world." It is only when we enter into the mystery of suffering and this equally mysterious thing called "forgiveness" that we can begin to come to live in peace in our not-so-peaceful world.

But forgiveness, in reality, is the heart's response of one who himself or herself has been forgiven. When we experience being forgiven, whether by God or by another, we can't help but play the game of life by a more merciful set of rules. As Jesus proclaimed, "She loves much, because she has been forgiven much."

24

"A soft answer turns away wrath, but a harsh word stirs up anger."

—Proverbs, 15:1

Etty Hillesum had "An Interrupted Life" (the title of her diaries). She died in a Nazi death camp in 1943. Despite the encircling doom she witnessed, she forgave her captors. She was not without harsh anger—or soft forgiveness—as she wrote: "And now and then I say nastily, 'They're all scum,' and at the same time I feel terribly ashamed…and [I say], '…there are still some good Germans, and anyway the soldiers can do nothing about it, and there are some quite nice ones even among them.'"

"God isn't finished with me yet."

—popular religious saying

One of the blessings of growing older is that one grows a bit more patient. "You finally find out that things don't happen overnight," quipped comedienne Phyllis Diller in a more serious moment. "So you're patient with other people and you're patient with yourself."

Indeed, some situations (and people) can be healed, it seems, only through divine intervention. But remember, you only have to be willing to heal. God can do the rest.

Pray for a willing heart…Dear God: It is obvious that "you aren't finished with me yet"; I am a work in progress. Help me realize that saying "I'm sorry" for an angry deed or outburst is one of the best ways to make peace.

26

"You can't stop the birds from flying around your head, but you don't have to let them build a nest in your hair."

—attributed to Martin Luther

We can learn a lot from the creatures about us, and the cycles and seasons of our lives. While we all have our favorite seasons, we must come to accept the sun and the clouds, the bluebirds and the vultures, the hot and the cold.

Lord God, teach me in the ways of nature to put aside the wintry season of my life, a season of bareness and bone-chilling cold and to seek the warmth of spring. Help me to move to forgive those who have harmed me and to forgive myself. Most of all help me to understand that your love sustains me in times of transition and doubt. Lord, I am tired of the hurt. I seek a new season. Amen.

"If we all got only what we deserved, only dogs would go to heaven."

—familiar saying

We know ourselves all too well, and if we believe in an all-knowing God, the logic takes us down the path to worry and trepidation: "How can a God who knows the real me still love and forgive me?" John Newton may have had the most concise answer of all: "Only these two things I know: I am a great sinner and Christ is a great Savior."

28

"Give us, O Lord, a humble spirit, that we may never presume upon your mercy, but live always as those who have been much forgiven. Make us tender and compassionate towards those who are overtaken by temptation, considering ourselves, how we have fallen in times past and may fall yet again."

—Dean Vaughan (1816-1907)

Meditate on the following familiar saying: "What you are is God's gift to you. What you become is your gift to God." Ask yourself: Am I becoming more peaceful and peace-filled? Do I blame my actions or outbursts on "That's just the way I am"?

Make a short list of the virtues you'd like to work on in your quest to become all that God wants you to be.

"Sin is the best news there is...."
—John Alexander, *The Other Side*

Columnist John Alexander tells us why he thinks sin is such good news: "Because with sin, there's a way out....You can't repent of confusion and psychological flaws inflicted by your parents—you're stuck with them. But you can repent of sin. Sin and repentance are the only grounds for hope and joy, the grounds for reconciled, joyful relationships." Now may be the time to say "I'm sorry"...to God, to another, to yourself.

30

"Whether the stone hits the jar, or the jar hits the stone—the jar breaks."

—Old saying

Whether we like it or not, jars get broken in this world we live in. Think for a few minutes of all the "jars" that have broken in your life; and all those that you yourself may have broken. Say a prayer of thanksgiving for the jars not broken, and a prayer of promise to fill empty jars with healing balm, with chicken soup, with over-the-brim love.

No doubt we have trampled upon lots of people in our lives, many of them unintentionally. There is also no doubt that it is a lot easier and more "natural" for us to find ourselves focusing on who was right, on getting even, or on how deeply we have been hurt, than on the more "divine" concepts of love, compassion, and the desire to be reconciled.

"The two sisters never apologized to each other, no matter what. Any apology would have been a patch of ground irretrievably lost."

—*Indiana Gothic*

Our habits have a way of clouding our vision, especially when it comes to anger and forgiveness. Perhaps you are feeling angry but aren't exactly sure why. Take a moment and jot down all the possibilities. Are you angry at a person? A circumstance? Yourself? God? Be as specific as you can. You may find you are mad at more than one thing. List them all and offer these targets of your anger to God.

We may feel as though we are "giving up ground" when we even start to acknowledge our resentments. But moving forward in practical and specific ways is the only route to real progress.

NOVEMBER

"Have mercy on me, O God, according to thy steadfast love; according to thy abundant mercy blot out my transgressions."

—Psalm 51

Writer Andre Dubus was a gun lover for years. He had carried a revolver with him for some 13 years. Sometime after he had lost the use of both his legs in a tragic accident, he came to the decision to get rid of his eight pistols. Wrote Dubus: "On the train I gave up answers that are made of steel that fire lead, and I decided to sit in a wheelchair on the frighteningly invisible palm of God."

And in an essay about the rape of his sister, he wrote: "But one bright day her anger and hatred will turn to white ash, and she will forgive him, the rape will finally end, and the man will truly be gone...."

Let us pray for that same steadfast grace and courage to blot out the great transgressions in our lives.

2

"I don't have any enemies. I've outlived them all."

—from a sermon on forgiveness

Forgiveness is hard. Sometimes we may wonder if we can outlast all the bad feelings. So many things get in the way of forgiveness: hurt, anger, pride, injustice, resentment. Yet most of us recognize forgiveness as a virtue to strive toward. The sacred writings of our religious traditions speak of it as essential to spiritual wholeness.

Rather than being some kind of favor to the person who wronged us, forgiveness is a key to unlock our own closed hearts. It frees us from being stuck in a past moment and old feelings. It relieves us of the burdens of anger and resentment. Forgiveness makes good soul sense.

"I don't get angry; people make me angry."

—anonymous

It can take some work to become aware of the things that trigger our anger. Writing in a journal can help; talking with a trusted friend is another good practice.

Changes in our body will give us clues. If we feel our muscles tensing, our stomach churning, our voice rising, it's likely that we're angry. And no matter how often we say, "No problem," our anger will be a problem until we first accept the ways we get angry.

4

"O Lord, remember not only the men and women of good will, but also those of ill will. But do not remember all the suffering they have inflicted on us; remember the fruits we have bought, thanks to this suffering—our comradeship, our loyalty, our courage, our generosity, the greatness of heart which has grown out of all this, and when they come to judgment let all the fruits which we have borne be their forgiveness."

—Prayer written by an unknown prisoner on Ravensbruck concentration camp and left by the body of a dead child

No human being can come to forgiveness without the grace of God, grace as clearly witnessed in this prisoner's prayer. Each day we have the option of accepting or rejecting the grace that is offered to us. Let us pray that we will accept it today.

"Just Walk Away, Renee"

—song from the 1960s

"My mother gave me one suggestion," said one friend. "She told me that simply by taking a half-hour walk everyday her mood swings, anxiety, anger all seemed more manageable."

Her suggestion is not, of course, to walk away from anger or resentment and get into a state of denial, but rather to give her anxiety and anger some perspective. When we get outdoors under the big sky, we can see that we are not, after all, in charge of everything. And that is good. Getting our bodies moving is proven therapy for body, mind, and spirit.

"We're all sinners—and if we're not we sure know we could be, with some luck."

—Matthew Kelty, O.C.S.O., Trappist monk

When we are feeling guilty and in need of making amends, (and who of us is not from time to time?) a simple prayer such as the following can begin the breakthrough: Dear God, Grant me serenity as I move forward in my life. Help me to be patient with the person I was yesterday and will probably still be tomorrow. With your help, I can make the most of today and face tomorrow with renewed hope, courage, and optimism.

"You burdened me with your sins, and wearied me with your crimes. It is I, I, who wipe out, for my own sake, your offenses; your sins I remember no more."

—Isaiah 43

Our God is so incredibly merciful that sometimes, it seems, we can be abusive of that mercifulness, and keep on sinning, using God's forgiveness almost as "a license to sin," knowing that our loving God will keep on forgiving us, no matter what.

We do well to remember our Lord's warning in John, 5:14: "See now, you are healed: sin no more, lest some worse fate befall you."

8

"Don't get mad... Get help!"
—slogan at counseling center

One way to keep from turning our anger or guilt inward is by publicly acknowledging our limits and weaknesses—to a boss, a spouse, a friend. It is often nothing less than surprising how people will respect our limits and respect us for admitting and clarifying them. God certainly respects our limits, and understands them fully.

Dear God, I know that peace and anger are opposite emotions; I cannot feel them both at the same time. Please help me remember that the anger I feel is not me. It is an emotion that is attempting to pass through me, deserving my attention and expression. But it is not me.

"Good actions ennoble us, and we are the sons of our deeds."

—Cervantes

Some of us grew up on the old saw, "Your actions speak so loud, I can't hear what you are saying." Thoughts, feelings, and ideas take place in the privacy of our heads or in our hearts. They can only be known as they are outwardly expressed.

A wise professor once observed: a person does not really know anything unless it can be outwardly communicated. Thoughts, feelings, and ideas must be put into words or some other form of observable behavior before they can become useful. Words or behaviors transform thoughts, feelings, and ideas into tangible realities.

Forgiveness is a wonderful idea. Forgiveness is a thought filled with warm and loving feelings. Yet, forgiveness must be expressed in reality. Forgiveness must be translated into love for ourselves and those who offend us.

10

"The Lord is merciful and gracious, slow to anger and abounding in steadfast love."

—Psalm 103:8

Sometimes we have to start "small." If we want to start our hearts on the way to forgiveness, we can start by accepting God's forgiveness for us. When we start taking small steps, we will find unexpected blessings coming our way.

If our own hearts are willing, we can believe along with Ezekiel 36:26: "A new heart I will give you, and a new spirit I will put within you; and I will remove from your body the heart of stone and give you a heart of flesh."

"Our God has a big eraser."

—Billy Zeoli

The above might be a good contemporary translation of the old saying, "To err is human and to forgive is divine." We know the saying well, and yet we go on, year in and year out, persisting in our pain, desperately in need of healing old grudges and wounds. What can we do to take the first step toward forgiving others or seeking forgiveness? Where is the road map to a happier life free from past heartaches and grievances?

By going deep within ourselves we can find true peace and joy in reveling in God's love, a love always ready, even anxious, to forgive.

12

"Am I angry? Of course, I'm angry. How can I see what I see, know what I know, feel what I feel—and not be angry?"

—modern songwriter

Anger can make us more productive, more powerful, more courageous in our character. And productive anger can change the world. Our teen daughter is angry about a domestic violence situation she is aware of in a friend's family. Her witness is evidenced in school essays and in speaking up wherever she can against abuse. Who knows—it may lead to a career in social work helping people avoid such abuse.

"Even God cannot change the past."
—Agathon

Sometimes the anger we experience in our life is anger toward others, toward God, or toward ourselves. Sometimes it is anger toward the community. Are there things in my culture, in society or in my own neighborhood toward which I harbor ill feelings? Do I feel I have been wronged by somc injustice or sin that is greater than any single act? Many people feel harmed by the prejudices, the lack of fairness or the competitiveness of the environment in which they live. Do we need to be healing?

Let us pray: Dear God, Help me to touch my anger and pain I may be feeling at the injustices of my culture or my society. Help me to challenge wrongs where appropriate and accept the things in life I cannot change.

14

"Do you want to be healed?"

—John 5:6

Faith in God is the key that can unlock the power of forgiveness in our lives. No, we can't be blamed for thinking and reasoning and acting and living in a limited, "this-world" basis. We are, after all, human beings. But we are also spiritual beings. Gathering in prayer with other believers and praying for forgiveness is a powerful way to allow the Spirit to lift us up and stretch us beyond our human-only capacities.

"Lord, if another member of the church sins against me, how often should I forgive? As many as seven times?" Jesus said to him, "Not seven times, but, I tell you, seventy times seven times."

—Matthew 18:21-22

Ancient tribal or clan justice, we note in our history books, permitted unlimited revenge for an injury. It was not only a time for "an eye for an eye," but a time for avenging one's transgressors seventy times seven times. In the Christian Gospels, Jesus turns this all around by proclaiming not unlimited vengeance but unlimited forgiveness. Why that's almost super-human, isn't it?

Writer William Menninger, in *Process*, sums it up beautifully: "Forgiveness is demanded by the very nature of man and woman. It is not only divine, it is also human. God commands it because without it we are less than human, with it we are more."

16 *"Talking nicely to God when your heart is full of anger doesn't fool God. It probably won't work well for you, either."*

—Carol Luebering

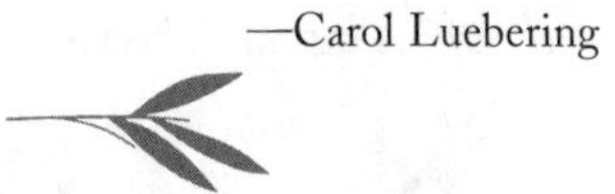

One woman says that she doesn't believe God would even recognize her voice if she weren't screaming, "What do you think you're doing this time?!" Join the company of biblical characters who voice their anger at God: The psalmists, Moses, Martha, the sister of Lazarus, Job, and many of the saints of old and not-so-old. See especially Psalms 6, 13, 35, 102 and 143.

Spend some time telling God in the intimacy of friendship exactly why you are furious. Yell at God, if that's what feels right to you. God can take it! God not only hears your outrage but shares it. Reflect on the times where it seemed clear that God came to you with understanding and compassion.

"As the first martyr prayed to you for his murderers, O Lord, so we fall before you and pray; forgive all who hate and maltreat us and let not one of them perish because of us, but may all be saved by your grace, O God, the all-bountiful."

—Eastern Orthodox Church

It is quite a revelation when we come to understand that the person who had the power to hurt us does not hold the power to forgive; we do. The power of human forgiveness is in the hands of the one who has been injured. What more God-like expression can there be than using this power to move proactively toward harmony and reconciliation?

It was St. Augustine, in his Confessions, who summed it up: "Let mercy triumph over judgment, for you...have promised mercy to the merciful."

18

"Everyone says forgiveness is a lovely idea until they have to forgive some-one."

—C.S.Lewis, *Mere Christianity*

How can we love those we don't even like? Only God can help us do that! And so we pray:

Dear God, give me the grit and power to face the events I hold in the buried parts of my heart. Give me the energy to be fearless in searching my memory and being honest and up front about what has injured or caused me pain in the past. I know I can do this with your help, with your love, with the support that you give me. Thank you for being with me as I open the book of my life. Amen!

"The simple truth is that if you are experiencing difficulties with significant people in your life, chances are that you will feel better if you talk to someone you trust."

—Hans Strupp

Talking to a friend about anger can be very healing. But try to find a friend who can be very healing and understanding—not just someone who will try to "egg you on" or "fix" things instantly for you. Sometimes we just need a good listener to open ourselves up to. One friend reminds me, "Opening up to someone can be frightening. Letting someone into your world requires that you let your guard down. But remember, talking about your pain is not a sign of weakness but a sign of strength."

20

"Faith is like a boomerang; begin using what you have and it comes back to you in greater measure."

—Charles Allen

Have you ever heard the similar "anger analogy" about being careful how hard you throw a ball against a wall; it will come back to you with the same force that it was thrown? Call it vengeance; call it retaliation; things come back to haunt us.

Taking just a few seconds, when angry, to ask ourselves, "What are the options here?" can be very wise indeed. We always have a choice.

"When you stand and pray, forgive anything you may have against anyone, so that your Father in heaven will forgive the wrongs you have done."

—from Mark 11

Who is your oldest friend? How has your friendship been forged in the furnace of difficult times and pain? Is there need for healing in this friendship? Are there unspoken apologies to be offered or accepted? What about your friendship with God? If this is a relationship in need of healing, a simple prayer such as the following can be a beginning:

Loving God, you are our friend. Help us to know that passion and suffering may be our way to genuineness and tenderness as they were for your Son, Jesus. Amen.

22 *"For it is in pardoning that we are pardoned."*

—Peace Prayer of St. Francis of Assisi

Long after the life of Francis, another insightful writer, George Herbert, expresses a similar sentiment to that of St. Francis. Said Herbert: "He who cannot forgive others breaks the bridge over which he himself must pass."

We all have seen movies and TV programs about people on death row, waiting for an eleventh-hour pardon from the governor. What an awesome thought it is that each of us is a governor, too, with the power to give a reprieve, to issue a pardon, realizing that in this way we ourselves can be pardoned.

It is only when we pronounce others unworthy of forgiveness and pardon that we block our own openness to being forgiven by God and others.

"You will never be an inwardly religious and devout person unless you pass over in silence the shortcomings of your fellows, and diligently examine your own weaknesses."

—Thomas a' Kempis

It was the same holy person who penned the words, "I had rather feel contrition than understand the definition thereof."

Revisit the story of the prodigal child in Luke 15:11-32, as you pray: Lord, help me to turn away from the dead ends of grudges, shame, and fear. Help me to take the first step to forgive others or seek forgiveness. I know this is not an easy road, God. I also know that you will be with me as I walk home to love and reconciliation. Amen.

24

"Confession is good for the soul."

— a Scottish proverb

It can be very healing to confess to ourselves and to God the truth in our hearts. Let your soul do the talking. It was Martin Luther who said it well: "When I am angry I can write, pray, and preach well, for then my whole temperament is quickened."

Let us pray: Loving God, Listen to my voice as I seek you deep in my own soul. Comfort and guide me on the path to forgiveness, healing, and growth. Help me to understand that the sorrow of the realities I might face within myself can be healed and strengthened by your loving presence. Amen.

"Mercy enables us to see things the way the other person sees. The other person may have in mind feelings which might be beyond ours."

—Archabbot Lambert Reilly, O.S.B.

In truth, sometimes it is really only a difference of opinion, of values, of upbringing, or styles of behaving. Only? Well…

Is it possible that the suffering we have experienced at the hands of others might well stem from their own vulnerability and insecurity? We react in hateful ways when we are hurt.

Lord, help me to see the pain of others, even pain that they may want to hide. Help me to understand that "woundedness" sometimes prompts wounding. Is it possible to clothe me in your boundless sympathy? Amen.

26

"On the year of jubilee you will have the trumpet sounded throughout all your land."

— Leviticus 25:2

It is one of the lamentable facts of life that we have all had the experience of being hurt by the words or actions of others. It is also true that we know that through our own cruel or careless deeds and speech, we have hurt others. The anger and pain that comes from having our feelings hurt or disregarded can be devastating and sometimes long lasting. In our hearts we know that there is no true peace in life until we are at peace with our neighbors, our friends, and the members of our families.

The ancient Hebrew people believed in the celebration of jubilees. Among the ancient Jewish people, the year of jubilee signaled a time when slates were wiped clean, when financial ledgers were balanced and those who were burdened with debt given a new start. We all need a jubilee now and then!

"O Lord my God, I cried to you for help and you have healed me!"

— Psalm 30:2

The most difficult step on the road to healing and forgiving past afflictions, grudges, and grief is the first step. We must embark by going deep within ourselves. In our hearts, in the silent recesses of our minds and imaginations is the secret place where memories are preserved, grudges nourished, and anger grows. It is sometimes exhausting, almost impossible, to look within and name hostility, injury, and disquieting memories.

How can I look within and be honest with myself about my anxiety, my hurts, my pains, and disappointments? Perhaps I can write in a journal some of the events or areas of my life that I need to confront, to name, and to heal.

28

"Get rid of all bitterness, passion and anger…Instead, be kind and tender-hearted to one another, and forgive one another, as God has forgiven you through Christ. Since you are God's dear children, you must try to be like him."

—from Ephesians 4

Father Lawrence Jenco, who suffered through 564 days of brutal treatment as a hostage in Lebanon, tells how he let some other words of St. Paul, touch him: "…The Lord is near. Do not worry about anything…" (Philippians 4:5-6). Now is a suitable time to ask the Lord's help to forgive as you are forgiven, and to love the enemy. God, after all, is the expert in forgiveness.

Make asking for divine help a daily habit. Include a prayer for the person who hurt you. You may find it difficult at first, but it will help you see the person with God's eyes.

"I utter my complaint and I moan and he will hear my voice."

—Psalm 55:17

There is a little story about a man who wanted to build a tower up to heaven in order to talk to God. When he sought advice about the best way to do this, he was told by a sage to get a shovel. The man ignored what he considered half-witted advice and started to build the tower anyway, which promptly collapsed. He returned to the sage who repeated his earlier advice, adding the words: "If you want to build a high tower to heaven, then you have to dig a deep foundation."

Facing anger, hurt, and forgiveness is really about growing up spiritually. Holding on to past injuries is a way of stifling our outreach to God. If we want to soar spiritually we must begin within ourselves. It may be difficult to face what we find there as we dig into the soil of our lives, but it is the only authentic way to grow.

30

"Forgiveness is a magnanimous gesture that increases personal power."

—Anthony G. Banet, Ph.D.

Nicholas Gage was only nine when his mother was executed by guerillas in Greece. Thirty years later, Gage, a *New York Times* investigative reporter, returned to Greece to track down the person responsible for his mother's death. Intent on revenge, he found at last his enemy alone and fast asleep. He stared at him for a long moment and then walked away.

Gage still lives with the pain of losing his mother. But to avenge her death, he realized, would have meant rejecting the legacy of love that was all he had left of his mother.

DECEMBER

"I will get up and go to my father."

—Luke 15:18

1

DECEMBER

Without a doubt, one of the most beautiful images of forgiveness and reconciliation in the Bible is the story of the prodigal son in Luke's Gospel. Luke gives us a powerful insight into the message of the Gospel when this "problem child" decides to turn the tide of his fortunes and seek reconciliation with his family.

In some ways we are all problem children. Haven't we all transgressed, missed the mark or had too much confidence in our ability to do it our own way? Likewise we all reach a turning point in life, a moment of truth when we decide that forgiving or seeking forgiveness is better than bitterness and grudges. Life is too short to wallow in the pigsties of guilt and depression. Maybe the moment of truth comes when we decide to forgive ourselves of secret sins we hold in our hearts.

2

"Lord, lead me in your truth."

— Psalm 25:5

Ernest Hemingway once said that his goal as a novelist was to write just one true sentence. Certainly he must have accomplished this goal many times over. The idea of writing one true thing can apply to our lives as well. But sometimes the truth is not easy for us to face. And sometimes we hide from it like adults playing hide and seek with children. We know where they are hidden but we pretend for the sake of the game. So often in our dealings with others we hide from the truth and say: "I am not angry" or "That did not hurt me." Inside, we know the truth is different because it is betrayed in every shying eye and sharp-turned word. Relationships wither in the chill of lies like naked blossoms assaulted by first frost and we are dishonest with others and ourselves and say nothing is the matter.

"I will hear what the Lord God will speak for He will speak peace to his people."

—Psalm 85:8

We all grew up with the axiom that "honesty is the best policy." Why, then, is honesty often so hard? We know that there are just some parts of our lives that we want to keep hidden from others, from God, and even from ourselves. We begin to develop clever lies about our lives. We say we are not hurt when we are really devastated. We claim to have forgiven others when we still hold grudges.

Healing and forgiveness can never take place in our lives as long as we are unwilling to admit that we are in need of them. Today is the day to face facts. Of course, this can be so rough. We have become too comfortable with the cover-up.

4

"Lord, teach me your way."

—Psalm 27:11

If being candid and true with ourselves compels us to face the facts about our lives and the reality of our relationships with others, it also forces us, as people of faith, to face the fact of God's grace at work. We know the anguish of life and we know its raptures. We know the chill of loss and the thrill of new discoveries. If we know those things, we must also know that it is the love of God that sustains us through times of trial and days of joy.

Grace is tangibly real in the wonder of the sunset, the bitter bite of snow, the cry of infants, the warmth of a hand. Grace is that serious intuition that we are not alone, even when we feel most separated from others and from ourselves. Grace is the impulse that leads us to reconciliation, to forgiveness, because it springs from the overwhelming generosity of God.

"O Lord, you have searched me and know me."

— Psalm 139:1

How is it possible for us to begin to forgive others, perhaps for bitter, devastating things they have done or said to us? What if we could begin by seeing others and ourselves for who we truly are: flawed and broken people. We have only to look around, to see the secret pain in the faces of those around us, the tear-filled eyes, the determined chin.

So many of us spend our years wearing masks of courage to hide our real feelings, our vulnerability, and our interior turmoil. Could it be true that our "enemies" and those who have hurt us could, for all their bravado and seeming courage, be really broken children, selfish and afraid in their hearts? Could it be so with me?

6

"O Lord Jesus, because, being full of foolishness, we often sin and have to ask pardon, help us to forgive as we would be forgiven; neither mentioning old offenses committed against us, nor dwelling upon them in thought, nor being influenced by them in heart; but loving our brother freely, as you freely loved us. For your name's sake."

—Christina Rossetti (1830-1894)

The idea of forgiving our enemies is one that is difficult for almost all of us to accept. Indeed, there is no way to reason ourselves to this conclusion. But forgiving our enemies is something that we are commanded to do—by Someone who forgives, but can forgive us only if we forgive others. We become capable of forgiving only at that point where we find it within our own heart to forgive.

"He has pity on the weak and the needy and saves the lives of the needy."

— Psalm 72:13

We have all used or heard the time-worn expression "Achilles' heal." We know it refers to our soft spots, those aspects of our personality or make-up that are vulnerable to the attack of sharp words, actions, or attitudes. In a more modern idiom we might refer to "pushing someone's buttons." Needless to say, people have a knack of finding the soft spots in others and using that realization to injure, to intimidate, or to isolate other people.

We know we have weaknesses, some that we try very hard to hide from others. There are secret places within ourselves we like to keep private and we are shocked when these darkened recesses are exposed to the light of day by someone else's careless revelation.

8 *"Refrain from anger and forsake wrath. Do not fret it only leads to evil."*

—Psalm 37:8

We all value our reputations and our good names. We spend our whole lives cultivating the good opinion of others through our behavior and our words. We are rightly devastated when our reputations and our integrity is called into question. Mean-spirited gossip, thoughtless conversations in the lunchroom at work, or an idle, unthinking word can destroy what we have so carefully built. We become angry with those who have hurt us. Hostility and resentment at others can be deep and long lasting. We hold grudges.

It is all right to be angry. Anger becomes a problem when we deny our true feelings and suppress our anger so that we treat others badly without fully confronting the source and reason for our resentment.

"The Lord is my strength and my might."

—Psalm 118:14

One of the real dangers of hostility and resentment is turning that anger on ourselves. Sometimes when others have bruised our egos or betrayed us we might begin to feel that it is our fault, that we are less-than-adequate friends, spouses, children, or parents. There is nothing more deadly than self-loathing. It eats away at self-esteem, tranquillity, and productivity. God did not mean for us to live this way.

Jesus said to his disciples, "I came that you might have life in the full." We are all made by the loving Creator as wonderful in our own right. We might do some things that are wrong but God still loves us. How can we fail to love what God loves, even ourselves?

10

"Great Spirit of the islands and countries, Father of our Lord Jesus Christ, we confess that we have seriously sinned in words, deeds and thoughts. Forgive us, please, and gently guide us in the ways of peace and love. Teach us to be more caring and loving to our families and to others, and to be more responsible in the task committed to us. Amen."

—Prayer from Karibati, Micronesia

Today, notice the evidence of God's constant grace: In the power of nature, in the foibles of others, in the rushing beat of your own heart. As you reflect, let the following lead your meditation:

O God, I am alive and it is your miracle that sustains me and encourages me on life's often perilous highway. I know I can face whatever life offers with your help and your constant presence.

"Their eyes stand out with fatness."
—The Psalms

An elderly lady lost her home and life savings in a scam engineered by a predator who became quite wealthy preying on helpless needy people. An ancient Psalm writer described such predators with "eyes standing out with fatness." As in our modern world, these predators were extraordinarily prosperous. They were so productive they became grossly overweight while others were at the point of starvation.

Predators generally care nothing for their victims. Their only concern is their own gain without regard for others. By most standards, they are remarkably successful. Do they deserve forgiveness? No! But that is why forgiving people are exceptionally special people.

12

"Things don't have to be perfect to be perfect."

—Christie Brinkley

None of us had a perfect childhood. But what is your most vivid "perfect" memory of childhood? And, while you're at it, what is a hurtful, "imperfect" memory that you would like to forget? Write it on a piece of paper and tear it to pieces, as you pray:

God, you know all my memories and thoughts. Help me to heal the memories of pain and disappointment and revel in the memories of fondness and celebration. Amen.

"The Law of the Lord is perfect."

—Psalm 19:7

No one has lived a dream life. Although television and movies may seduce us into believing that life can be flawless and beautiful, we know that real life is not a sit-com or a romantic movie. In life we have to deal with real blemishes, dandruff, less-than-perfect homes and cranky friends and family members. While the Law of the Lord is perfect, at times that law is written with convoluted lines. In spite of this truth some of us still expect perfection. We become annoyed or frustrated when life is not as it appears on television and in advertisements. That is not to say that we should not have high expectations and strive after great goals. It does mean that if we look too hard for the pot of gold, we might miss the rainbow of life, which can be ravishing even in its imperfections.

14 *"By the rivers of Babylon – there we sat down and there we wept when we remembered Zion."*

—Psalm 137:1

Memories are like fresh bread, given a bit of leaven and a little time to rise, they grow way beyond their earliest proportions. Happy memories can sustain us through difficult times, the memory of a lover's gentle touch on our cheek, or the smell of fresh starched laundry drying in the summer sun. We cherish our memories of treasured grandparents and friends, of old teachers and pastors.

Painful memories, too, can haunt or taunt us throughout life, memories of brusque words or unconsidered actions, memories of childhood hatefulness or adolescent anxieties. Sometimes we need to heal our lives of hurtful memories that may have grown out of proportion and come to dominate us in ways of which we may not even be fully aware. First, we must face them, as old friends or adversaries.

"Turn to me and be gracious to me, give your strength to your servant."

— Psalm 86:16

God did not mean for us to waste our lives. How many people do you know that go through life, not really paying attention, not really living? Certainly all of us get bogged down at times in trivialities, in meaningless pursuits and even in wrongdoing. Sometimes, though, we can lose our way through real adversities that we face, the sickness and death of a loved one, our own illness, financial difficulties or broken relationships. There are real troubles in life. How do we face them? Are they occasions for tearing away of our confidence, our bliss or our faith? Could it be that the pains we have suffered, even at the hands of others, could be opportunities for growth and for maturity?

16

"Lead me in your truth and teach me."

—Psalm 25:5

You do not need this book to tell you that life is a journey. Sometimes the journey is smooth sailing. Sometimes the way is a bit more jagged. It is never colorless. You also do not need this book to tell you that some of the most momentous experiences of life are the stormy ones. Growing pains are a part of life but there is no growth without change and a little discomfort. So often, however, we try to minimize this aspect of life by covering up adversity with drugs, alcohol, or inappropriate relationships. To live fully is to face hardship. To face hardship is to grow and mature. The question is not a life without trouble but rather a life in which we are able to courageously face trouble and doubt.

"A true friend sticks closer than one's nearest relative."

— Proverbs 18:24

Relationships are complex. In the history of a friendship, a romance, or a marriage there are moments of tender intimacy and serious betrayal. Doubt and confidence walk hand-in-hand. Our friends, our loved ones are our source of greatest comfort. They are also the very ones that can wound us the most. We may feel estranged from close relatives, yet know real and lasting intimacy with our friends. One thing is certain, however, relationships advance in the crucible of adversity.

True intimacy is cultivated in times of shared trials and need. Can we use this insight to help us understand the need to forgive others, to use times of hurt, doubt, and even betrayal to grow to a more full life?

18

"Let me hear of your steadfast love in the morning, for in you I put my trust."

—Psalm 143:8

We might like to think of our lives as fascinating and full of escapades, but most of us are faced each morning with the daily round of routines. We wake up, we eat our breakfast, we go off to work, and we come home. We eat, we sleep, we pray. Most days are like every other, filled with joys and laughter as well as little disappointments.

We somehow believe that God is not God unless there is drama, thunder, smoke, the crashing of waves. We fail to see God in the little things and hold out for the special effects. Yet God is not in the earthquake, but rather the still small whisper. Sometimes healing old pains and injuries depends on the right vision. I cannot wait for God to hit me over the head before I decide to get my act together.

"Lord let me know your ways."

—Psalm 25:4

People frequently seek the advice of their pastors because they are having difficulty discerning God's will in their lives. What does God really want me to do with my life? Should I consider marriage, children, the single life, or a religious vocation? Does God want me to consider a new career path or a change in residence? Sometimes it can be difficult to sort out these perplexing questions, even when we are sincere in our desire.

One thing is certain, God always wills forgiveness and reconciliation, because God is by nature forgiving and reconciling. We can never be wrong when we choose to forgive or seek forgiveness.

20 *"We resist, after a fracture, the sacrifice of re-setting the bone."*

—Thomas Merton, from a talk to novices

God, I know that I can never be cured if I do not admit that I am hurting. I know that I can never find or seek forgiveness if I will not acknowledge the injury. I need your help, God, to be honest and truthful with myself and others. I seek your face O God and your truth. Amen.

In heartfelt honesty, with God at your side, write down in a journal some of the truths of your life that you have tried to evade because their memory is too aching. God is with you.

"He made the storm be still and the waves of the sea were crushed."

— Psalm 107:29

God is the creator of all things, the aching, gnarly oak's mighty arms, the amber of the evening seashore, the whisper of a lover's words, the etching of the wind by butterfly's wings. God also does with nature what He wishes, including our human nature, so raw and naked, so sleek and radiant as it is. In the Gospels, Jesus' mission is to show God's vigor in confounding nature, to stifle storms, to overthrow disease, to vanquish death itself.

So often we think or hear in the face of human moral or physical frailty and thoughtlessness: "O so and so is all too human." Perhaps the truth is that sometimes we are not human enough. God has the power to modulate our natures, weak and poor as they can be, and forge them more like his own; good, forgiving, "transformative" in themselves.

22

"O Lord, pardon my guilt."

—Psalm 25:11

Mulling over past bruises and insults often leads to feelings of guilt and shame. We are embarrassed to face them or to admit that the hurt and pain happened in the first place. Occasionally we also confuse these emotions of guilt and shame. Guilt is that part of my understanding that comprehends that I have done something wrong. Guilt convicts us and keeps our consciences on the right course. Shame is different. Shame is pernicious and ruinous. It turns the "rightness" of guilt to self-loathing. If we fail to acknowledge our wrongdoing (and we know when we are wrong) then we can begin to believe that we are bad people. Or worse, we can try to convince ourselves that those who have wronged us are bad people. The source of guilt must be faced and eradicated for shame to be subdued.

"For everything there is a season."
— Ecclesiastes 3:1

There is nothing more certain than the seasons. The frigid beauty of winter is the seed ground for the verdant exuberance of spring. The excess of spring gives way to the sweltering reality of summers that decay into the chromatic astonishment of autumn. It is also true of the seasons of our lives that one time gives way to another.

The author of Ecclesiastes said it best, "For everything in life there is a season." Sometimes we realize without prompting that the time has arrived for action. This is the season to put away old grievances, to seek forgiveness and to forgive. The coldness of our grudges and grievances must give rise to new life, a life that can only spring forth by forgiving the faults and frailties of others and ourselves.

24

"We like someone because. We love someone although."

—H. De Montherlant

Perhaps today is the day to take an inventory of my real feelings: About my family members, about my neighbors, about my friends, about my coworkers. Let the following be your prayer today:

Lord, help me to understand the bitterness and resentment I may harbor against my friends, my coworkers, my neighbors or my family members.

"Do not forsake me when my strength is spent."

—Psalm 71:9

When I was a child we had a Christmas tradition. We had a little plaster statue of the baby Jesus that we placed under our Christmas tree each year. We loved our little Jesus doll and took good care of him. He was an important part of our lives. Then one year, tragedy struck. Our dog, in a particularly aggressive mood, decided to play with Jesus and tore his little plaster leg from his body. The family was so upset. We did not know what to do with this broken, mangled Jesus. Should we throw him away? Should we try to repair him? In the end we decided to leave him as he was, broken and wounded. Somehow he seemed to be Jesus even more that way.

How do I face my own "woundedness?"

26

"While he was still far off, the father saw him and had compassion; he ran and put his arms around him and kissed him."

—Luke 15:20

The character of the father in the parable of the prodigal child is complex. On the one hand, he can stand in for all those from whom we need to seek reconciliation. On the other hand, he can represent God, the one who is always willing to take us back and pick us up. Luke unveils for us in this parable the exquisite image of the father who runs out to greet his son, even though the boy has proved an ungrateful wretch.

The question for us in this whole drama of forgiveness and reconciliation is: How do we respond to those who seek forgiveness from us? If we are in need of forgiveness in our lives, from others and from God, certainly we must learn to first be skilled at forgiving.

"His elder brother was in the fields."
—Luke 15:25

The third character in this little play is in many ways the most troubling. The older brother refuses to have anything to do with the celebration initiated by his younger sibling's homecoming. The problem for us, of course, is that there are times when we can relate to this young man's dilemma. He has done everything lawfully. He has not dishonored his father, his family, or his legacy and yet he is not receiving any attention.

Often we can become jealous of the generosity which God seems to show toward others, particularly those we might not view as model citizens or disciples. Can we learn to forgive God for being so generous?

28

"In the days to come all will have been long forgotten."

—Ecclesiastes 2:16

We all know the old adage "forgive and forget." We also know that nothing is that simple, but certainly the motivation to forgive and reconcile involves something more; that is the desire to put the past in the past. How open are we to forget past transgressions? Do we still hang on, nursing our wounds even when forgiveness has been sought and granted?

Likewise, we do not wish to fall victim to what we might call "doormat syndrome." That is conveying the belief to others that we are easy marks, that we can be treated in any way whatsoever and always "forgive and forget." Actions have consequences but candid and forgiving hearts yield consequences as well.

"Depart from evil and do good so you shall abide forever."

—Psalm 37:27

Life is filled with choices. Many of them are inconsequential, almost meaningless. What kind of soap should I buy this week? Others are more important. Should I get married or not to this person? Nevertheless all choices involve some sacrifice. If I choose this road, I must forget about these possibilities. Every choice is also a loss. Sometimes we must learn to acknowledge and move beyond these losses.

What do we lose when we make the choice for forgiveness and reconciliation? We lose our old hurts, our grudges, and our fears. Ironically, sometimes we have become so accustomed to living in the pain and suffering that we may not know how to live without them. How can I depart from mourning and misery and activate the goodness and the example of God within me?

30

"Create in me a clean heart."

—Psalm 51:10

Reconciliation is more than just the ability to forgive and forget. It involves something positive, something proactive. Reconciliation implies creating a clean heart and forging new opportunities in relationships. If we believe that growth is tempered by adversity and that time of pain and doubt can help yield new harvests, we must uncover the good, even in past hurts. Reconciliation means not only moving beyond, but also moving toward.

What are the opportunities for growth in my experience of forgiving someone close to me? How can I employ the wisdom of having been forgiven to change my life, to realize a new opportunity?

"Now is the acceptable time. Now is the day of salvation."

— Second Corinthians 6:2

These short meditations on the need for forgiveness and reconciliation in our lives have brought us full circle to the celebration of jubilee. Jubilee happens when we wake up one morning and realize that our lives could be so much happier and more fulfilling if we only did a little housecleaning. Jubilee happens, when at the end of the day our reflections encourage us to open our hearts to the needs and hurts of others and seek peace. Why should we continue living in sorrow and misery when happiness is only a step, a word, a letter or a phone call away? When should we open ourselves to the life God intends for us? Now is the acceptable time. Now is the day of salvation. Today is jubilee!

References

Gravitz, Herbert and Bowden, Julie D. *Guide to Recovery: A Book for Adult Children of Alcoholics.* Holmes Beach Florida: Learning Publications, Inc., 1985.

Leaves of Gold. Clyde Francis Lytle (ed.) Williamsport, PA: The Coslett Publishing Co. Revised 12th printing, 1963.

Lewis, C. S. *Mere Christianity.* New York: The MacMillan Co., 1953.

Lifton, Robert Jay. *The Nazi Doctors: Medical Killing and the Psychology of Genocide.* New York: Pocket Books, 1960.

Peter, Lawrence J. *Peter's Quotations: Ideas for Our Time.* New York: Bantam Books, 1977.

Schell, David W. Illustrated by R. W. Alley. *Forgiveness Therapy.* St. Meinrad, IN: Abbey Press, 1993.

Schell, David W. *Getting Bitter or Getting Better: Choosing Forgiveness for Your Own Good.* St. Meinrad, IN: Abbey Press, 1990.

Sunrise to Starlight. May Detherage (ed.) New York: Abingdon Press, 1966.

The Treasure Chest. Charles L. Wallis (ed.) New York: Harper and Row, 1965.